Man, Environment & Development in Himachal Pradesh

To
HEIRA

Man, Environment & Development in Himachal Pradesh

A.R. KHAN

INDUS PUBLISHING COMPANY
NEW DELHI

First published in 1996
by Indus Publishing Company
FS-5, Tagore Garden, New Delhi

ISBN 81-7387-036-5

Published by M.L. Gidwani, Indus Publishing Company
FS-5, Tagore Garden, New Delhi 110027, and printed at
Elegant Printer, 38/2, Mayapuri Indl. Area, New Delhi.

Contents

Preface

Techno-genesis has been going on alongwith socio-genesis. Man in its pursuit of development has constantly been interacting with the environment. The intensity, mode and type of interaction determine the resultant scenarios.

Himachal Pradesh, which has been a fragile ecosystem, of late, is recording significant pressure of man's demand—which is rising relentlessly. Man's action, too has definite pattern. In economies, drawing directly from nature the pattern is discernible as coterminus with the idios type of ecosystem. Diversity of economic activities may ultimately be drawing from the same environment. It is on this premise a system of man's idios environment and unique development is evaluated in the present book.

Development level evaluation is having under consideration not only man's endeavour of constant improvement in its lot but also what is vouchsafed by nature to it. It is imperative thus to include in study the natural set-up from where all the resources—substances of satisfying human wants—are coming from. The regions which have recorded greater development due to resource endowment or whatever historical reasons are different from those where resource development are at nascent stage or underdeveloped. Himachal Pradesh is one of those regions where natural constraints have held it back and more so the present "gadgets of development" do not fit in well. This way it presents a case in itself for evaluation. However, findings can also be used for furtherance of the concept to the similar man-environment milieu. Mountain-man, mountain-environment and mountain-development options have all high degree of similarity. It is only the resultant development which may, to some extent, be different in different cases.

India is a welfare state. The concept of development in case of India is different from the development hypothesis of the West. The consideration of mere economic variables for level evaluation may not be enough because it will only be presenting part of the picture. Quite a few economic ventures are counter-productive yet adopted and advocated for and are included in the final analysis of development level evaluation. The consideration of a special venture having different scale of operation is difficult and may also be confusing. The spatial scale thus has been used for developmental level evaluation and it is no doubt the level on which man interacts with the nature. The availability of information at district level with respect to development and a respectable level for understanding development vis-a-vis man's role and impact on spatial environment has led towards their consideration. There are certain activities which do not reflect the impact on a man-made spatial unit but have their own zone of impact and interaction. The climatic zones which have led towards the birth of classic economic activities are other spatial units which can be used for understanding of the interaction of the three, i.e., man, environment and development. In a situation such as Himachal Pradesh no doubt one has marked variation in terms of the three at district level but the differences are even significant when man's similarity and environmental homogeneity is there and development then can be evaluated at "agroclimatic zone". The major economic activity being agriculture —which is also the product of the environment and is a sector where man, environment and development interact with each other and that is visible at agro-climate scale.

The interaction of man and environment and the resultant development is not constant as all the participating elements themselves are dynamic. A development level assertaining once and for all time to come may not be possible, hence all the evaluation in the present book is based on specific frozen time-space framework. However, if one goes by the concept of cumulative causation, the chances of furthering the situation are possible. But it is as long as the negativities in the environment do not set in, as they may turn out to be a very significant factor for fragile ecosystem such as Himachal Pradesh taken as a whole.

The element based consideration of development or interaction has mixed results. A region may not be developed for all the elements at the same time such as it may be comfortable with GNP average but poor in social variables such as human resource development. This goes a long way affecting the genesis of interaction of the three. It is also based on serious problem of the consideration of' different factors for the same end, i.e., development where man's actions are different and also varied is the endowment and responses of the environment. Not to miss, the development being considered similar in each case has its own limitations.

The injected growth initiatives of the government have brought about considerable confusion in interaction evaluation. The economic factors introduced from outside affect the man's relationship with the environment and consequently the level of development may not be the product of local factors. It is with this perspective that a separate treatment of the government's initiative of development has been considered in this book. This should be understood in the light of the fact that they may appear outside factors to begin with but after setting in the environment they may cause strain on the local system, at least to begin with.

The interaction of man with environment has caused various pockets of development and zones of problem in Himachal Pradesh. It has a close relationship with the expectation of people from the environment and the fragility of it as such.

This is proved by elements based on consideration of development at both man-made spatial unit, that is district and also nature-man scale of agroclimatic zones considered in the book.

The author is grateful to a number of people and institutions who have directly or indirectly helped at various stages of preparation of this book. Shri V.P. Gupta has always been encouraging and his philosophical interpretation has helped the author in understanding similar things in different perspectives. His inter-disciplinary training tacitly runs as undercurrent in this book. The author owes gratitude to Shri R.B. Singh and Shri Ras Behari Prasad Singh. There is a long list of persons who have always been very kind and helpful—Dr. S. Mohapatra, Shri T.P. Singh, Shri T.S. Rana, Shri P. Yadav, Shri B. Ali, Shri S.N. Singh, Shri Daljeet, Shri Manoi, brother Masoom and Shri Kulbhushan from Manali are only to name a few. The author also has a sense of gratitude to Shri Prem Nath and Shri Sher Singh for their help in typing the manuscript. Shri M.L. Gidwani, the publisher, his interest in the Himalayan Studies has also been a very significant factor. The author owes a gratitude to him.

At the end I must also include the deep sense of gratitude that I have for my family for everything they have provided me.

A.R. Khan

CHAPTER 1

Man, Environment and Development

Man and nature have been at war with each other since the dawn of civilization. The nature through its shield of diversity and vagaries has always tried to defend itself and man with its cultural and technological advancement has always been on the attack. Man wins in most of the cases and makes a habitable world, even at a place where most of the natural facilities are at the lowest. Nature, if it cannot stop "cultured beings" to exploit it, does take revenge and its fury can put man in a great fix.

The boundary of ecosystem somewhat sticks around a cultural boundary or vice versa. The mountainous ecosystem has a typical habitational practice within its own limit. Again, within Himachal Pradesh—a typical mountainous state—one can observe marked differences in terms of habitational practices or in other words, a cultural and developmental boundary very close to agroclimatic boundary. The economic development does reflect the natural endowment of a region, at least in a developing society like that of Himachal Pradesh.

The study of developmental status in geo-academic circles is still in its infancy. The economists, on the other hand, have made quite an advancement but their fallacy of undermining space as a factor has many a times led them to erroneous conclusions. Evaluation of level of balanced eco-development is never possible by undermining space component. There have been quite a few models of development analysis in economic spheres but they have never accommodated space as an important factor. The adherence of such models has led to imbalanced development as the resources of development and the beneficiaries both have quite strong spatial reflections.

Conceptual framework

The process of economic development has always been for increasing the income through technological changes in production. In this process the attention has been less on inter-regional development differentiation. The growth experience of developed countries in their earlier phase of economic development led to the belief that there is near inevitability of high rates of urbanization for rapid industrialization process. India, an underdeveloped country after gaining political independence from the colonial rule looked forward to the 'received' growth experiences of the developed nations for initiation and adoption and naturally tended to emphasise on urbanization and industrialization strategies for economic development.

The heavy concentration of economic activities in a few urban centres was expected to create "ripple effect" of growth throughout the nation. This emphasis led to the neglect of dominant economy, mainly rural areas which even today is a major source of economy and remains the supplier of the most important human life requirements. The 'centre mode' assertion that "disequilibrium is built into transitional societies for a start" (Friedmann 1966) is a never ending process. The causation factor of "ripple effect" is much strong at the centre than their distribution all around.

The anthropogenic activity stems from the basic structure of economic set-up and cultural milieu in a particular region. Himachal Pradesh, in its earlier stage of economic development, has been largely drawing from the natural endowment that is bestowed by nature. The secondary and tertiary activities have very limited expression in the form of selective industrial outcrops and restricted developed economic nodes which invariably are also political nodes. This is a common feature prevalent in economies which are in their earlier stage of development. The anthropogenic impact evaluation, as the relationship with the nature goes on towards remote side which is also indirect, is a difficult exercise. However, for an economy which is largely stemming out of natural bounty is relatively easier. It is also so, because the activities are limited keeping the impact towards lower side of the scale.

The primary activities usually have cultural base because of their longer exposure to the society and as it is also with the economy of India that one generally notes a cultural apathy existing for secondary, that is, industrial activities. This draws from the fact that larger share of population is engaged in primary activities. The present study also largely focuses on the primary activities acknowledging their cultural imprint for the evaluation in the form of anthropogenic impact analysis.

The criteria for adoption and conception of development has always been varied. It also varies with the philosophy that guides the adoption of developmental activities as well as the models used for developmental activities. In the recent times the conception of development is also found tainted with the fact that they are adopted for a particular motive. Depending on the large varieties of expression and development it becomes very difficult and confusing to come out with a uniform criteria which can give an idea of status of development even if they are taken independent of the factors affecting it or the events affected by them. As Indian economists have adopted an *idios* philosophy of development which is restricted from using the western models for status evaluation of the economic development that has taken place in any part of our country.

Welfare has always been a significant aim which an economic philosophy accounts for with great restrictions. However, this welfare act has a primary goal as we had decided to attain economic development on socialist lines. Variety of counter-productive exercises at times are taken up only in the name of welfare. These counter-productive exercises no doubt are very much part of our economic development exercise but their treatment through western models become difficult. However, realising the limitations posed by adoption of unique development model, one is mostly drawn towards utilization of western economic development models with their inherent limitations. The western economic models with their true economic criteria of development evaluation like GDP, GNP, etc. are used but their clubbing with the environmental impact presents a better picture in the sense that at what "real cost" the present development status has been attained. And this has been tried through the adoption of anthropogenic impact evaluation that is the "true economic development" and is coming at what cost to the society which is still in its juvenile stage of growth.

The constant effort of putting up the growth of economic indicator unit not reflected in development is considered in its project denotation. Statistical evidence had shown a secular rise in national and per capita outputs of the developed countries, the same could now serve for the underdeveloped countries as a double criterion, viz., as a measure on the basis of which a line could be drawn between the developed and the underdeveloped countries, and as an objective function to be maximized so as to enable the latter group of countries to catch up with the former at some future date.

Thus growth of national and per capita output emerged as a 'rational' index of development and underdevelopment, because that is what seemed to be suggested by the development experiences of the already developed economies.

With the consideration of per capita income or output as indicator of development it was assumed that development and welfare went hand in hand. It, however, may be refuted at two levels, i.e., at the economic development level and the welfare adoption level. The developing economy like India where growth habits in many parts of the country are still at infancy and also in a situation where density of population is low due to natural reasons, the consideration of per capita output may lead to erroneous result. Again the distributive justice must also draw from demand and supply situation and mere consideration of output indicator which might give in to a situation where simple services are to be provided at very high cost. Again the inherent problem of factor optimality is of great concern for welfare evaluation as it might ignore geographical consideration of welfare. Thus, various inherent problems may lead to the discontinuation of such approach in geographic developmental studies.

The one to one consideration of development, welfare and distribution is of great significance which cannot be explained through the independent consideration of either economic sector or geographical space or sociological welfare parameters. The comparison does not end here. Various, economies have their unique analysis of sub-economies which operate within their idios admixture. Hence, a broader framework for comparative evaluation was needed *ab initio*. The development which is of area, people and growth habit must also be considered in the same light. The levels of development of each one of them may be matched amongst and shades of development band may thus be identified. A larger and intensified detailed effort throughout the hills leads to highlight further the development linkages between people and development attained, leisure, sacrifice and integrity of development expression, etc. Perhaps the greatest weakness of the per capita GNP as an indicator of development achieved is that it does not obviate whether the process in a given real world situation which is class or mass-oriented. In other words, this criterion of development does convey a sense in the context of relative poverty, but fails to provide any idea of the level of, and the rate of change in the case of absolute poverty.

Another major problem related with the welfare condition and adoption of economic indicator is that in the early stage of development, as may be the case in developing country like India or any sub-economy like Himachal Pradesh, there exists hardly any relationship between growth in GNP and income equality. The earlier period records growth of GNP without equal growth in equal income distribution. The trickle down effect of economy still holds validity in the minds of planners who initially created inequality in supply resources to a region and assumed that its growth will take care of development of the region. There is no automatic trickle down of benefit of development due to weak income linkages within the economy. Thus, keeping in view the above mentioned hypotheses a constant need was felt to extend an ideal type which takes stock of the situation i.e., natural resources and population status and then extends an explanation which indicates development measuring method tailored, according to the particular stage, the economy is put to question.

The rapid growth of population has caused pressure on natural resources which to some extent is taken care of by the advancements made in the technosphere. The lack of technological advancement and somewhat faster rate of growth of population has made the geospheric system of developing nations look deplorable. The situation is aggravated when and where the relationship between the resource mobilisation and the environment is direct and also in condition when the latter is fragile and vulnerable. The finite resources have a limited scope for supporting a definite strength of population within a given framework of technology. The advancement of technology, thus, is the major guiding principle. Nevertheless, pragmatically speaking it has to yield to the stretch of depleting resources.

A particular resource, if considered in a broader perspective, is a component of the larger ecological system of that area. There are of course, various constituents of the ecological systems but the consideration of geo-ecological system broadly includes the parameters (or constituents) which have direct relation/bearing on natural systems. The symbiotic relationship between the constituting parameters make them a functional system and the encroachment in one is ramified over other constituents and the system as a whole, keeping in view the fact that a particular resource is finite and is a constituent of the broader ecological system. The technological experimentation of exploitation are costly and the expectations of the human-kind has always been on an increase, it seems but necessary that one must come out with the broader principles before the situation gets altered and the beneficiary becomes the victim of their own need and deeds. The geo-ecological principle gains much more momentum and weight in Indian mountainous situation whose encroachment can lead to disasterous implications for which the nation is tight-pressed by technological advancement to alter and get away with. The limits to growth were a major guiding principle for last few decades but now is waning out. The geo-ecological principle many a times stem out from the physical resource base using persons as numbers. They were quantified in terms of carrying capacity explanation etc. Further growth in principle of geo-ecology has stress on quantitatively exploring the concepts of Quality of Life (QOL). Earlier it was stated as Standard of Living (SOL), which is a ratio between economic development and population.

Now with the advent and deterioration of environment the quality of life has become economic problem, i.e., one must account for the problems that are invited due to blind adoption of methods for economic development.

It appears wholly logical, therefore, that if a concept of development is to reflect both growth as well as equity so that it is truly "socio-economic" in character, it must be based upon criteria which can measure changes over time in the aggregate output as well as the existing production potential of the economy, and also throw adequate light on the emerging style of its development. While the former would take care of the 'growth' or 'economic' aspect, the latter would account for 'equity', 'distribution', or 'social' aspect of development. This, therefore, is the *raison d'etre* behind a synthetic approach to the concept, criteria, and measurement of what has been called 'genuine' or socio-economic development (Sharma, '85).

To be succinct about the measures of development performance evaluation in terms of level, it appears that no unitary approach is sufficient. Even for a sub-economy like Himachal Pradesh, various sets of factor of social and economic importance in relation to the endowment and population, need to be considered. The impact of human being adds a new dimension to the whole situation and the spatial expression of impact form an integral aspect of developmental level evaluation. The dearth of adequate statistics is another major impediment which also restricts the adoption of most favoured approach for development level evaluation.

The resource-population relationship is dynamic and it is consequent upon different development levels. The quest for development ushers in greater utilisation of resources and if the resources in question is straight out of nature there is greater chance to pay heavily for it. As far as the situation of impact is concerned if one considers that what Malthus (1926) said, was right about progression of subsistence to be in arithmetic form i.e., 1-2-3 and population in geometric 2-4-8, then a new dimension of impact can also be added to the anthropogenic impact which will grow as 8-64-512 and so on. The explanation is that when population grows the anthropogenic impact does not grow in the same fashion as its growth (in most of the countries) is the result of two factors i.e., decline in death rate (or addition of dependents) and growth of fertility (or addition of dependents). These factors demand for the development in standard of living which in turn accelerate anthropogenic impact on environment. In this situation presence of anthropogenic impact is felt less amongst dependent population (below 15 and above 60) and active anthropogenic impact is felt by population between 15 and 60 years who constantly strive to better their living standard and impact upon surrounding.

The ever-increasing anthropogenic impact for economic development has reached an alarming stage where situation, if not checked, may even go out of control leading to catastrophic situation as productive forces have a tendency to form counter-productive situation after certain limit. It is also realised that in developing nations where majority of people are engaged in primary sector the carrying capacity of the region is less unlike advanced economies where the services of other tertiary activities enhance carrying capacity which is also sometimes aided by external carrying capacity.

For making a better living a high economic development was a logical consequence and realising the high potentiality man initially concentrated on high production by enhancing the technology (impact tool). But time has come and it may be realised that higher production is taking a tacit toll in the sense that it began receiving diminishing return and sometimes the activities even turning counter-productive by rising environmental management cost.

Man and Environment has been in the centre of discussion right from the age of Blache. However, the consideration of its interaction has been changing and the present work adopts man as an agent with a capacity to cause certain impact (anthropogenic impact) and that impact-genesis is also tried to be traced through economic behaviour or to say for economic development by man.

Early studies on man-environment nexus

G.P. Marsh, an American Scholar, in his one of the earliest statements related to the nature and extent of changes to the natural environments due to human interventions, stressed that nature could not rehabilitate itself. Man's increasing dependence for his survival on natural resources has had negative and chain impact on the ecosystem and stressed that developmental activities should be designed to minimise disturbances for creating harmony with nature. Most of the studies made by Sauer in forties concentrated on the way in which human activities have altered the natural environment to create a cultural landscape. In this context, one of the most important dialogues on man-land relationship was convened by the Wenner-Gren Foundation and the National Science Foundation in an inter-disciplinary symposium held in 1955 at New York with the focal theme—Man's Role in Changing the Face of the Earth. Sauer and other contemporary geographers actively participated in that symposium. The symposium realised that man often becomes irrational in the treatment of the environmental resources. Because of irrationality in resource use, man may create a grave situation for himself which may ultimately lead to negative impact on his own base of subsistence. Danassauers also examined man's impact upon the landscape in bio-geographical perspective during sixties. Bouwer (1985) emphasized the relationships between geography and the study of environmental problems. The list of geographers who have developed and contributed to environmental impact studies associated with human use of the resources is quite long.

In fifties much of geographical works concentrated on quantification and quantitative explanation and development-environment nexus in geography was no exception. But soon it was realized that the inclusion of man and quantification for various preference studies and impact analysis was falling short of the target and hence qualitative and ecological approaches once again came to the forefront of such analysis.

As mentioned above, man and development had certain localisation but in the larger framework certain generalization in the form of developed nation and developing nation may be traced. Despite the fact that environmental problem is rampant in both the developing and developed nations; their genesis is different. The magnitude of problem also varies with it. The present study of man-environment relationship and its impact evaluation is a hunch in the same direction.

Survey of developmental studies

The beginning of the study of environment problems arising out of different economic activities was first made on global level during 'Stockholm Conference' in 1972. During this conference the shadow effect of development was felt and advised to different governments of the world to identify their developmental activities which are non-detrimental to environment. This conference also gave rise to the development of several sub-committees to monitor the guidelines provided therein. The UNESCO Committee established in 1973 came out with findings that the life support system is recording very heavy pressure on most of the mountainous regions of the Developing World. The report of MAB (Man and Biosphere), another committee has pointed to certain activities which lead to environmental degradation in the field of soil, flora, fauna, etc. J.D. Ives (1981) has also arrived at the conclusion that the developmental activities of man many a times contribute adversely to ecologically fragile zones like the Himalayas. Bochet (1983) after evaluating the various mountain systems of the world has opined that situation in the Himalayan foothills is degrading fast and calls for serious effort before the situation gets worse beyond repair. The symposia, 'Mountain Population Preserve' (1983) and 'Mountain Development Challenges and Opportunities' (1984) held at Kathmandu were the extension of various UN sponsored programmes to highlight the environmental problem and need for environmentally viable economic development strategies. Various seminars and workshop from time to time have greatly emphasised on monitoring the human pressure, anthropogenic impact and development activities, so that the ecologically viable planning may be extended where irrepairable losses are being made to the flora and fauna in the name of economic development.

The geography of spatial inequality or development disparity has emerged as an important branch of geography and several scholars both in the developed and developing countries of the world have attempted to evaluate the criteria and techniques to identify and determine the development disparity in different parts of the world.

The United Nations and World Bank have also identified some basic variables to determine the socio-economic level of development. For better understanding the contributions of Western and Indian scholars can be reviewed separately by identifying their works.

Western works

Several theories and models have been propounded from time to time to identify the levels of development. The locational theory of Thunen (1926) provided a framework for socio-economic development. Weber's (1929) theory of industrial location was yet another important contribution in this regard. The Central Place Theory of Christaller (1933) provided a base for spatial development through settlement system. Haggerstrand's (1952) model of 'Spatial Diffusion of Innovations' explained the processes of development. Barnet (1952) prepared non-monitory index of development to focus the attention of international disparities. Losch (1954) developed a modified theory which is based on Christaller's idea. The 'Growth Pole Theory' of Perroux (1955) and 'Cumulative Causation Theory' of Myrdal (1955) examined the factors responsible for regional imbalances. Hirschman (1958) and Ullman (1958) also attempted to identify the levels and strategy of development.

The concept of development and social welfare was first developed in geography during sixties as mentioned earlier. Some geographers used quantitative methods to measure the social well-being and development disparity. Berry's study, who applied principal component analysis to measure the level of development, is very significant in this regard. Barren *et al* and Cairncross (1961) also discussed the factors and stages of economic development. The social system integration approach of Friedman (1961-64) is yet another important contribution to study the economic growth. Williamson (1965) attempted to evaluate the concept of social welfare and economic development and evolved the much discussed technique for measuring the inequality. Harper *et al* (1969) suggested a recreation based economic development model and growth point concept.

Adelaman and Morris (1967) used Factor Analysis for making international comparisons in development. The works of Boudeville (1966), Thompson (1966), Hansen (1967), Harmansen (1969) and Schaffer (1969) were also significant in measuring the levels of development and development disparities.

There are several attempts which have been done by scholars to measure the levels of economic prosperity but there has been no unanimity on the use of indicators and the methods to be employed. In the beginning, the infant mortality was taken as important indicator which was followed by income, health, housing condition, levels of education and gross domestic products, etc. Coate *et al* (1977) identified some basic variables such as income, health, shelter, nutrition, education, leisure, security, stability and quality of life, etc. and used multiple component analysis to measure the level of social well-being.

A few other works, which have been done in this area and are worth mentioning from theoretical and conceptual view points, are those of Kuklinski (1972), Harvey (1972), Drewnowaski (1974), Clason (1974), Slator (1975), Backer

(1976), Stohr (1977), Smith (1977, 79), Hinderink (1978), Streeten (1980), Barcelon *et al* (1980), Johnson (1981), Stohr and Taylor (1981), Heggins (1981), Gillesple (1983), Bromely (1984), Browett (1984) and Rondinelli (1984). These are classical works in their own rights. Bronger's (1986) work on Andhra Pradesh (India) is an important contribution in this field. He too has used principle component analysis for treating the variables. It may be mentioned here that before these sophisticated techniques came to play major role, the Lorenze Curve, Gini Coefficient, Ranking and Aggregate Method and Score Transformation were very important measurement techniques of marginal disparities.

The economic development evaluation have been undertaken by Richardson and Gordon (1978) with the help of Economic Base Model. The Economic Base Model have recently gathered quite a significance among theories of developmental economies, partly because of their incorporation in regional econometric model (their appeal being a direct link from the greater to smaller region within the standard macro-econometric framework). The two most common methods of measuring the base are the variants of the location quotient method and the minimum requirement method. For incorporation of the present model in terms of the developmental status evaluation in the agroclimatic zone is possible through use of the central place hierarchy. Through this it can be evaluated that the economic base multiplier is a special case of the central place multiplier and the multipliers tend to be larger in the high order places. The method used by Richardson and Gordon has been slightly different in the way that they used space explicitly, and economic base multiplier impact decay over distance negative exponentially. Both the ways of using economic base model are supposed to lead to the same conclusion.

Nijkamp and Van Felt (1986) have been the pioneers of qualitative impact analysis in a regional context. They gave argument that impact analysis has to attempt to assess all relevant preselected and expected consequences of external changes in a system within a given time period. This implies that anthropogenic transformation in terms of spatial environmental, political and cultural, are as relevant components for the system as the standard economic variable. Nijkamp has also used soft data (qualitative) for drawing inferences which were ultimately quantifiable. Multi-dimensional scaling methods used to transform ordinal data into cardinal units. Other methods were based on the ideas that different ordinal variables may reflect and measure a common phenomenon. This model also makes use of replacing several variables on the criterion of the principle maximizing homogeneity.

Indian works

In India too efforts have been made to identify the levels of development by using different variables. One of the most common variables which has been used quite frequently is income. A special concern over regional disparities was emphasised during second Five Year Plan, and following programmes as corrective measures were taken up:

1. Special attention was given to under-developed areas.
2. Priority was given to agriculture, irrigation and community development works.
3. An extra attention was drawn towards backward regions by way of providing water, power, transport and communications, etc.

The efforts were also made to get the theoretical input regarding the inter-regional and intra-regional disparities. The study of Ashok Mitra (1961) has been pioneering in this field. He used simple ranking and adding method to delimit the regional disparities. He employed as many as 30 variables to explain the spatial pattern of development. Nath (1964) adopted the same method to highlight inter-regional disparities in India. He used 14 variables. Rao (1973) selected 15 variables and processed them to identify the basic dimensions through Principal Component Method for the backward states of India. Pal (1975) applied same method which merits special consideration to evaluate the spatial pattern of regional imbalances. Ganguli and Gupta (1976) also identified the levels of living indices for 15 states of India. The components considered were, nutrition, housing, health, education, clothing, scarcity and environment. Hem Lata Rao (1977, 85) used Factor Analysis for measuring economic disparity among the states. She opines that the regional disparities have declined over the period of time and process of convergence has already set in. This may partially be attributed to the policies and programmes of the Five Year Plans which continue to endeavour for balanced regional development.

India, with 77 per cent of its people living in nearly 5.76 lakh rural nodes of different sizes, has always had very good prospects for research in rural geography. It is, however, surprising that most of the quality researches in this branch of geography are still being produced by the Western scholars. In spite of the fact that the phraseology of Rural geography was used and conceptualized by N. Subrahmanyam back in 1926, it did not witness any satisfactory progress until about the next two decades. Prof. E. Ahmed had been the pioneer at his work on rural settlement, and rural population in Bihar and elsewhere set a tradition and opened some new vistas of research. The village and land-use survey reports published by Prof. S.P. Chatterjee, Prof. V.L.S. Prakasha Rao, Prof. G.D. Deshpande and Prof. Mohd. Shafi further strengthened the academic roots of rural geography. During the period of 1952-82, works heavily centred on settlements-origin, growth, functions, typology, pattern, morphology, housing and building materials, and rural service centres, etc., without taking into account the socio·causal correlations and spatial linkages. Although the study of rural settlement retain their importance within the subject today, rural geography has expanded over the last decade to encompass other lines of enquiry such as the systematic study of rural transportation, employment and housing assessment of development policies in rural areas and attempts to develop theory and methodology in rural geography (Pacione, 1983). This trend which started in the west in 1970s ensured the study of rural development a prime position in 1980s. In India the location specific district plans for integrated and balanced development of the rural areas were emphasized by the planning committee in the fifth Five Year Plan, which considers 'development block' as primary area unit for local planning (Misra, 1985).

Rural development in India has a long history. The first attempt in this direction was apparently made in 1885 with the objective of bringing immediate relief and development to the rural areas of Baroda. In 1926, a Royal Commission on Agriculture was appointed to examine and report on the conditions of the rural economy in general and of agriculture in particular. In 1935, rural reconstruction centres were organized at several places. In 1943, the "Grow More Good Campaign" was initiated for raising food production. Soon after independence, several states initiated rural upliftment programmes, inspired by the ideals of Mahatma Gandhi. But all these efforts had one major shortcoming. They were more or less adhoc and uncoordinated efforts without any conceptually broad-based strategy. The stress of secular planning by economists sometimes appears to be coming at the cost of regional imbalances. Those economic developments at times may not finally come down to the poorest of the poor violating our conception of socialist state. The large size of the country and diversities extended alongwith, make it an ideal situation in which shifting to the policies more integrating in nature appears viable. A large resource base existing in the rural areas for very long time have remained untapped largely because of the lack of infrastructure and plans to integrate resource at their level for an overall development coming in the form of balanced regional development. Despite the fact it has several benefits, it no doubt suffers from the problem of integration at different scales. Not unaware about the demerits involved in this, economists in India found it worthwhile to experiment and embarked upon strategy of community development on 2nd October, 1952. Thereafter, many programmes like Intensive Agricultural District Programme (1961), Small Farmers Development Agency (SFDA), Marginal Farmers and Agricultural Labour Programme (MFAL), Drought-Prone Area Programmes (DPAP), etc. were launched. Most of the programmes undertaken during the five year plans were sectoral, centre-drawn and unrealistic. These programmes did not take into consideration the basic needs, larger interests of overall welfare of the rural people at the local and the lowest level, and also lacked the co-operation and participation of the local people including their resources, technology and talents. Ultimately, it was considered, that Integrated Rural Development would be the most feasible and viable framework for spatial Rural Development. It is a multi-sector, multi-level and multi-section approach in a dynamic perspective. As a multi-level concept it encompasses rural development at various levels in the spatial hierarchy, such as the viable cluster of village communities, block and district. As a multi-sector concept it encompasses development in various sectors and sub-sectors of rural economy such as agriculture, industry, education, health and transportation. As a multi-section concept it encompasses socio-economic development of the poorer sections of the rural population such as landless labourers, artisans, small farmers, marginal farmers, scheduled castes and scheduled tribes.

In developing countries, especially in those like India, in the planned process of growth, high priority has been given to the emancipation of poverty, reduction of inequalities and elimination of under privileged. As has usually been observed, due to lack of a coordinated and integrated approach the impact of planning and development has turned out to be uneven and sporadic, creating regional and social imbalances. Dholakian and Iyengar's work is an outcome of detailed and intensive study of Ghazipur Tehsil in U.P. with regard to its overall development. The authors take stock of its resource potentials, both physical and human with a view to provide employment opportunities and more so a better standard of living to the people. The optimum utilization of land and irrigation potentials, proper arrangement of agricultural credit, provision of better health, education, marketing facilities and development of transport system, applying growth centre concept and adoption of appropriate policy framework, have been visualised as the effective approaches/strategies for the development of the area.

A research monograph by S.P. Mishra (1985), advocates the most pressing problems of the country related to rural development. The utilization of the resources with special reference to land and water, agriculture and farm technology, rural industries, etc. has been properly evaluated. Different rural amenities like health, education, transport and communication, and financial institutions as well as the spatial arrangement of service centres and their hinterlands have been competently dealt with. After a concrete analysis of the aspects of rural development, an 'Integrated Rural Area Development Plan' centering in the idea of inter-sectoral condition and multi-level planning, has been presented to bring the entire activities into single system of self-generating growth cycle. The study emphasizes the plan implementation machinery in which the revamping of Panchayati Raj institutions and individuals representing all the sections of society should be given equal participation to gain the real benefits of different programmes.

Another study by Sudhir Wanmali in 1987, focuses on government policy to its impact on a system of service provision in rural areas of India. It is critical on the current urban-industrial-based models of rural development in India. It notes that such models have failed most of the time because the requisite mechanisms for spatial development were missing from (but were assumed to exist) in such models. The author demonstrates that it is possible to view rural development as an entirely rural process involving development of agriculture, rural service system and agro-processing. The book analyses a dynamic situation spread over the period 1968-82 in two different structural areas (irrigated and dry) involving locations, spread and use of rural (government sector) and ritual services. It is shown that not only they have the regions grown, although differently, but also that households have benefited from an increasingly accessible rural service system in India. Implications of the study for regional policy, district planning and design for a distribution system of goods and services are noted.

Archana Gaur, in 1985 studied the Koil Tehsil in U.P. from the perspective of Integrated Rural Area Development by analysing its resources and form. She formulates an Integrated Rural Development Plan which is based on rural resources. It further attempts to intensify the basic planning units in the tehsil

Goswami and Gogoi, 1989, make an attempt to study the Integrated Rural Development Plan with reference to Asia and notes it to be unsatisfactory.

Dinesh Rai, 1988, undertook a study in five selected blocks of Varanasi district and found that Integrated Rural Development Plan had a favourable impact on income generation despite its marginal effect.

Regional planning has become a part of modern National Planning and has created a new place for contributive research in Geography. It deals with the delineation of hierarchy of regions based on the physical and human resources and an appraisal for a balanced and integrated development. It is a significant concept serving as the means of regional development and resource utilization on scientific principles and equitable distribution and utilization at the regional level. Regional planning is important in its approach to the development of undeveloped and developing areas, rural and community development and the location of industry to solve the problems arising from unbalanced growth.

The works on regionalisation can be grouped into three divisions namely: (1) Division of India for geographic purposes, which exhibits the similarity and difference of areas, (2) Regions delineated for relative purposes, and (3) Regions delineated for resource development.

The first attempt at regionalisation of India was by L.D. Stamp in 1922. He divided India into three macro regions and 22 sub-national regions. Continuing the effort of L.D. Stamp, W.A. Wood prepared an outline map published a little later by J.N.L. Baker. The two schemes were in close agreement. In 1939, Pishawala criticised Stamp's scheme and published his own scheme of physiographic divisions of India. Following the empirical tradition of Baker and Stamp, O.H.K. Spate attempted a more detailed breakdown of regions in 1954.

Development-environment nexus

It was the environmentalist who began to question the premise that an ecologist could continue helter-skelter without eventually incurring severe environmental losses. Elaborating on this theme economists like Kenneth E. Boulding attributed much of the man's spoiling of nature to his inadequate frame of perception. In *Beyond Economics* written in 1968, Boulding claimed that man still saw his natural resource base as a limitlessly exploitable frontier. The "cow boy" economics, as Boulding termed it, did not account for environmental costs, i.e. "externalities" which are part of the "true" cost of production.

The concept of "externalities" developed by Marshall and elaborated by Pigou, remained a theoretical abstraction until Kapp published his 'Social Costs and Private Enterprise' in 1950. Kapp documented the environmental costs of business activity. His basic thesis was that the maximisation of net profit by micro-economic units (like entrepreneurs) was likely to reduce the income generation of other units and of the society at large. In short, he claimed that conventional measures of the performance of an economist, were misleading since they neglected social and environmental costs. J.W. Forrester came to the same conclusion in his 'World Dynamics'. In this book Forrester shows in a complex non-linear system the optimisation of any sub-style would go against the welfare of a large section of the population.

The controversy over development not only continues to expand but it is also reappearing in the form of a debate, that is, ecology versus economics. While environmentalists maintain that the economic growth must be curtailed for the basic reason that ecological balance forms the pre-requisite or the pre-condition for any "actual" development to take its form. The concepts through which a particular region is developed by the allocation of resources at the cost of surrounding region and eventually expecting the growth habit to trickle down, does not have many real world comparison. Referring to this concept Peter Passel and Leonard Ross in their famous book "Retreat from Rich: Affluence and its Economies" argue in favour of accepting the faster rate of growth to take care of the less privileged lots of the society as the growth fruits trickle down. The basic debate arises when the environmental factors are brought in picture. When the intensified and intentional supply of additional resources to a particular region in the name of faster economic growth is made, the ecological balance is bound to be affected.

It is very fashionable by economists to include environment while accounting for economic growth. The open market strategies give rise to generation of surplus capital and finally accumulation. The accumulation of capital also opens vistas for intensified utilization drawing heavily from the natural bounty. Acting as a system, intensified utilization also opens room for depletion sometimes coming in quick succession and at times coming slowly; nevertheless sure to follow. The situation can be viewed from two angles, that is, first if the utilization is intensified and environmental consequence follow, or secondly, the intensification is lacking but the zone under question is environmentally fragile, that is, major effect can be noted through smaller interactions. The first situation is more common to developed world whereas the second situation is typical of developing economies and it is still more expressed when one considers it in ecologically fragile zones like Himachal Pradesh.

In regions of ecological fragility and developed economies the percentage of shared resources is higher. This also exhibits that free goods are readily available and hence more vulnerable. Nicholas G.R. in his book "This Entropy Law and the Economic Process" has drawn the attention towards the problem in which open resources and vulnerability to environment operation increase in entropy, that is, loss of control is higher in the situations when the resources are commonly owned. The poor organisation and usually long time cycle of nature readjustment process invite several factors to set in before the real readjustment takes place. It is not just that if we only revert to a situation where ownership of resources is more defined and accept that the situation is improved. As a matter of fact any change, if large in scale, will also give rise to the problem of the scale of disaster.

The conception of eco-development as a model has been accepted both by developed and developing nations and here a detailed stock-taking of the natural resources, relationship with the economic activities and impact of large economic operations are seen before one conceives of any developmental project. The eco-development concept is also taken as more viable model of development where scarcity and fragility are the norms of the resource. The Himalayan regions no doubt were earlier taken as a sleepy economic region now can boast of a fast economic development at par and at times faster than the national average for many of the indicators. However, this must be viewed in the perspective of fragility that exists. The faster rate of development has started taking its toll, and various regions can be identified where economic activities are turning counter-productive. The highland-lowland interactive mechanism also presents a situation in which environmental vulnerability seeps downstream. The uncontrolled resource exploitation upstream has resulted into various environmental problems in the Gangetic belt where majority of the population of our country reside. Despite the fact that our scientists from physical, natural and humanities streams have been drawing constantly to come down with a model which is viable for the Himalayan region and also takes care of environmental ramifications, majority of the models fall flat when they have to face the problems like growing population, rural-urban migration, high pressure on land, infrastructural development, forest fires, drying streams, or, to sum up, the anthropogenic expressions.

It thus becomes necessary to have an account of detailed resource base which attracts and gives room for multiplicity of economic activities. The resource base appraisal and its sustainability is the task that should be taken at the second stage and this must also be based on the fact how much pressure in terms of human resource a particular region has to sustain. The present work on anthropogenic activities serve as a model for impact evaluation because it is found to be most penetrating, in an economy which is at developmental stage, on resources which are largely commonly owned, and environment, as a whole, which is but a very delicate balance of all these factors.

CHAPTER 2

Land and People

The State of Himachal Pradesh lies between 30° 22' 30" north to 33° 13' north latitudes and 75° 23' 24" east to 79° 00' 50" east longitudes. The State has maximum stretch in east-west direction at about 310 kilometres. The north-south expansion accounts 310 kilometres. It encompasses a total area of 55,673 square kilometres.

Himachal Pradesh is recognised as the VIIIth macro level region of India belonging to the Himalayan mountain region.

The State is beset between Kashmir Himalayas in the north and north-east direction and Uttar Pradesh Himalayas and the Upper Ganga plain in the east and south-east direction. In the south-west it meets with the Punjab plains.

Culturally, this State is bounded in the north by Jammu and Kashmir, in the south-west by Tehri Garhwal and Dehradun districts of Uttar Pradesh, in the south by Ambala district of Haryana and in the west by Ropar, Hoshiarpur and Gurdaspur districts of Punjab. In the east, however, it has a common international boundary with Tibetan China.

Historical perspective

Himachal Himalayas has had a long and chequered history from the time of Hominid presence to this day. It presents an interesting mixture of various cultures which has left an indelible mark on its landscape. Due to its long history and presence of human settlement, Himachal Pradesh offers an ideal case where long time anthropogenic impact can be evaluated.

Dawn of civilization to British occupancy

The history of Himachal is an ancient one and goes back to the dawn of civilization. The evidences from various excavations of Himachal Pradesh proves the existence of Hominid, an ape like being in the east of Hari Talyangan village in Bilaspur district in Himachal Pradesh. The pre-Vedic history of human settlement of the Himachal Pradesh presents an interesting facet being located on the fringe of Indus Valley civilization (between 3000 B.C. to 2500 B.C.). The earliest human race to be found in Himachal were the Kols (Proto-Australoid), also called Dasyus. In the post-Vedic period they were referred as Kinnars, Yakashas, Kirats, etc. When the Aryans entered Himachal they assimilated with the various tribes of the State. They adapted themselves to a distinct society of family and village life. One finds mention of present day Himachal in various Vedic literature. In the Puranas Himachal is Jalandhar Khund of the Himalayas. Panini refers several hill tracts like Trigarta, Kulunte (Kullu), Mandamati (Mandi).

In the later centuries the Hill Chieftains accepted the suzerainty of the Dravidian Empire, the Kushans, the Guptas and the Kannauj rulers. It was during this time that the new class of Rajputs emerged and settled mostly in the Northern and Western India. In Himachal they succeeded in subduing the local Barns, called Ranas and Thakurs to establish their own principalities such as Trigarta, Kullu, Chamba, Nurpur, Suket, etc.

During the Mughal period there was not much interference from them except for Akbar the Great, who sent Todarmal to annex the area. Otherwise during the time the Mughal rulers and the local chiefs of the hill states made some mutually agreed arrangements which governed their relations.

After the Mughal Empire started losing their grip over the Indian states, there rose a new warrior class in the Himalayan region known as the Gorkhas and spread throughout the Western Himalayas. Subsequently, in the 19th century Maharaja Ranjit Singh subjugated most of the Himachal territory which eventually came under the British rule. The British rule lasted for almost one and a half century. This area witnessed some improvement in the sphere of transport and communications, education, trade and commerce, during British rule.

With the first war of independence of 1857, the whole of India was united in the effort of ousting the foreign power from the country. The impact of national movement was also felt in the Himachal. The struggle of people gave rise to several movements like the protest against the 'Begar' (forced labour) giving rise to the 'Praja Mandal Movement'. This era also saw the rise of various popular leaders like Dr. Y.S. Parmar, Pandit Padam Dev, Comrade Ramchandra, etc.

Independence and thereafter

After India attained Independence on 15th August, 1947, all the princely states were being integrated into the Indian Union. Thus, in March 1948, thirty princely states of Shimla and Punjab Hills merged together to form Himachal Pradesh in the form of a unit which was formalised on the 15th of April 1948. Bilaspur, another princely state, which remained a part 'C' state was merged with it in 1954.

After the State Reorganisation Commission, appointed in 1953, examined the question of reorganisation of the States of the Indian Union, the legislative assembly was replaced by territorial council in 1957, but this political set-up was proved to be a failure in terms of economic development of the State.

Subsequently, in 1963 the territorial council became a legislative assembly and Dr. Y.S. Parmar was appointed as the Chief Minister of Himachal Pradesh.

Hill areas, which included districts of Shimla, Kangra, Kullu, Lahaul & Spiti, which were part of British India in 1947, which did not fall under the princely rule were left out as part of Punjab State. The year 1966 saw the division of Punjab on linguistic basis. While the Hindi-speaking areas in the plains formed a separate Haryana State out of it, the hill Hindi-speaking areas were integrated with Himachal Pradesh. Thus this state got its logical present status with its area and population in November 1, 1966 (Kaushal, 1988).

After 1966, the demand for 'Himachal' statehood gained momentum and finally in December 1970 the Parliament passed the bill to make Himachal Pradesh a full-fledged state. Late Prime Minister, Mrs. Indira Gandhi, inaugurated the state on 25th January, 1971 and Dr. Y.S. Parmar was sworn in as first Chief Minister of the new state of Himachal Pradesh.

Physiography

Himachal Pradesh presents a rugged, undulating topography. The whole state is mountainous. Thus presenting a complicated scenario. One may find four broad stratigraphical zones from south to north:

1. Outer or Sub-Himalayan zone
2. Lower Himalayan zone
3. Higher Himalayan zone, and
4. Tibetan or Tethys Himalayan zone.

This mountainous state ranges between 450 and 6,900 metres in altitude. The general elevation increases from south to north and from west to east direction. There are parallel ranges and valleys with numerous rivulets and rivers draining the region. The southern and Outer Himalayan Hills are low and composed of unconsolidated deposits, which are subject to severe erosional activity. These Outer Himalayas have several Duns (valleys)—Paonsan Valley, Balh Valley (Sundarnagar), and Kangra Valley. North of the Outer Himalayan zone lies the Lesser Himalayas which rises in elevation towards north. In this region there are east-west parallel valleys with an exception of Kullu Valley.

Among mountain ranges Dhauladhar and Pir Panjal are major ones. In the further north lies the Great Himalayan Zone. This is the highly eroded and glaciated area of high mountains with deep gorges. The Great Himalayas range from 1500 to 6000 feet traversing the state from north-west to south-east direction. There are ranges like Kangra 5248 metres, Baralacha 4512 metres, Kanzam 4551 metres, Parang 5548 metres and Pin Parbati 4802 metres, separated by passes formed by the rivers Spiti and Beas. Zanskar range makes the eastern boundary with Tibet. This range is cut through by river Sutlej making Shipkila pass.

Drainage and watershed

Himachal Pradesh possesses numerous rivers due to its mountainous terrain. The main rivers which drain in the eastern part are Yamuna, Tons and Giri flowing towards the Gangetic plains. Sutlej, Beas, Ravi, Chandrabhaga (Chenab) and Malung drain in the western part to meet with Arabian Sea.

Himachal Pradesh forms an integral part of the Indus-Ganga basin. The catchment area of all major rivers are snow-fed.

Among major rivers Sutlej commences from the uplands of Tibet and enters Himachal Pradesh at Shipki La Pass, where it is joined by the river Spiti. Its catchment areas within the state is about 20,000 square kilometres. Chenab has the largest volume of run-off in the state. It flows for about 120 kilometres within the state with a catchment area of about 7500 square kilometres, which is mostly barren and thinly populated. The Ravi flows for about 108 kilometres within the state with a catchment area of about 5450 square kilometres. The Beas has a length of about 250 kilometres in the state with a catchment area of 13,000 square kilometres, which is of great economic significance. The river Yamuna has a catchment area of about 11,000 square kilometres within the state represented by Liri-Bata and Tons-Pahar river system. The Malung is a glacial terrain in the north-east of Lahaul and Spiti which later join Indus through Tsarap Chu and Zanskar rivers. The rain-fed rivers of Ghaggar and Markanda mainly drain part of lower Himalayas and Shivalik zones.

TABLE 2.1

River systems and watersheds

S. No.	River systems	No. of watersheds
1.	Chenab	23
2.	Ravi	71
3.	Beas	66
4.	Sutlej	57
5.	Yamuna (Liri having 35, Bata a direct drainage and Tons Pahar 40 watersheds)	85
6.	Soan	31
7.	Sirsa	17
8.	Ghaggar	6
9.	Markanda	9
	Total	365

Geology

Himachal Pradesh is mountainous state mostly comprising tertiary rocks. In the southern part of Himachal, from west to east there is great thickness of detrital rock-clay and conglomerates. North of this belt, there are mainly granite and other crystalline rocks having unfossiliferous sediments. The southern Spiti and upper Sutlej region rocks are mainly metamorphic with intermittent granite. But in the northern part of the state, the complete sequence of the fossiliferous palaeozoic and mesozoic strata, lays bare. The Giumal sand stone with yellow ground sand stone and quartzite overlie in the northern Spiti valley. In northern and north-west of it, is found the grey limestone with soft grey calcareous shales. This area is rich in fossils and has many well exposed sections.

Geology of the state is very complex as it has been subjected to severe tectonic movement in the past. Rocks of various ages lay exposed. The pre-Cambrian rocks are very dense, hard and crystalline with absence of fossils. They are igneous and metamorphic in character. The Palaeozoic, Mesozoic and Cenozoic rocks are soft fossiliferous and are composed of sediments of diverse facets. At several places volcanic rocks are also exposed as in the case of Mandi where they are known as Mandi Traps. The igneous rocks such as granites, etc. form the core of mountain. The metamorphic rocks of Pre-Cambrian age include gneisses, schists, marble and slates, etc. The sedimentary rocks belonging to Palaeozoic, Mesozoic and Tertiary age include sandstones, shales, limestones, conglomerates, breccias, etc.

Soils

The soils of this state vary according to its altitude and climate. Various organisations and geographers have classified the soils of Himachal. The Agriculture Department of Himachal has classified the soils into five classes, viz.

1. Low hill soil zone—up to an elevation of 900 metres
2. Mid-hill soil zone—between 900-1500 metres
3. High hill soil zone—between 1,500-2,100 metres
4. Mountainous soil zone—2,100-3,000 metres
5. Dry hill soil zone—found in very high altitude in Lahaul and Spiti, Pangi and Kinnaur districts.

The soil units respond greatly to the physical set-up of the state and correlate with the climate, vegetation and relief, to a greater extent. The soils of Himachal Pradesh have been grouped into further eleven sub-order associations. In the Udalfs and Udalfs-Ochrepts associations, the soils vary between high base status soils of humid regions and shallow black, brown and alluvial soils of northern regions. They are found mainly in north-eastern parts of Chamba district, southern parts of Lahaul and Spiti district, central parts of Kinnaur district, central and eastern parts of Sirmaur district, eastern half of Bilaspur district, southern Mandi and Kullu districts and northern tip of Solan district. Orthents-Ochrepts soil associations are recently formed soils having shallow black, brown and alluvial characteristics. They are found mainly in central parts of the state, covering, the eastern Kangra district, eastern Hamirpur district, northern half of Mandi district, western and southern Kullu district, northern Shimla district, western Kinnaur district and south-eastern Lahaul and Spiti district.

In Ochrepts, Ochrepts-orthents, Ochrepts-psamemts, Ochrepts-orthents-ustalfs, Ochrepts-orthents-rockout croks-orthids and Ochrepts-orthents-*Utalfs* associations, the soils are shallow black, brown and alluvial of recent origin. Also some sandy soil, alluvial soil and arid region soil with certain development are present. These soil associations are found mostly in north-western and south-western parts of the state and also in the south-eastern tip of Kinnaur district. It covers the south-western Chamba district, most of Kangra, Solan and Hamirpur district, north-western Mandi district, whole of Una district, western half of Bilaspur district, northern Sirmaur district and south-western Shimla district. The Udolls soils are similar to the Tarai soils of humid region and are found in the north-eastern tip of Chamba district and northern part of Lahaul and Spiti district except the north-eastern tip. The glaciers and snow capped soils are found in very high altitudes in the north-western, north-eastern and south-western parts of Lahaul and Spiti district, eastern part of western tip of Kinnaur district, northern tip of Shimla district and eastern parts of Kullu district.

Forests

Himachal Pradesh displays great diversity on forest growth due to variation in elevation, rainfall, soil and other physical set-up. The recorded forest area accounts 37.6 thousand square kilometres, but the actual forest cover accounts 11.8 thousand square kilometres which is 21 per cent of the total geographical area of the state.

Sal forest is found in southern part of Paonta Sahib tehsil. Subtropical scrub forests such as bamboo, khair, sissu, flourish in low altitude areas of Kangra, western Bilaspur, Nalagarh and Kandaghat parts of Shimla and central western parts of Mandi. Subtropical scrubs and lower and upper pine forests are found in central Sirmaur district. The south-eastern parts of the state records scrub forests.

Himalayan moist temperate forests grow in Chamba and northern Kangra district while Himalayan moist wet temperate forest is limited to eastern part of Mandi Sadar Tehsil. The most important species of trees are Deodar, Kail and Oak. Himalayan temperate forest with predominance of Deodar and Kail are seen in Dhauladhar ranges, central Chamba, Karsog Tehsil of Mandi, Kandaghat Tehsil of Shimla and adjoining areas. Himalayan dry temperate forest is predominant in the catchment areas of Chenab river and along the upper basin of Sutlej river. Dry temperate forest (High level blue pine) and sub-alpine forest such as Fir, Birch are extensively found in south-western Chamba, south and central Kullu and in Mahasu region. Most alpine scrub and dry alpine scrub, coniferous types of forests are found in high altitude areas of northern Kulu, eastern parts of Rohru and in Kinnaur district. In Lahaul and Spiti and Kinnaur districts where rainfall is scanty, vegetation is scarce and is confined to river valleys only. Elsewhere bare rocks are found.

Forest based industries in the state have provided employment to 36,975 workers. The largest number of workers engaged in the exploitation of forests have been recorded in Kullu district 17,503.

Minerals

Himachal Pradesh is rich in mineral wealth but proper survey is still needed. According to the Geological Survey of India, there are deposits of limestone, gypsum, dolomites, pyrites, clays, mica, building stone, slate and lead in various parts of the state. Despite the fact that the state is rich in mineral resources, the present use is limited to quarrying of limestone, building stone and slate. Besides, for the construction of roads, housing and roofing, stones and slates are obtained in plenty from all over the region at various places. Rock salt is obtained from Mandi. Limestone is found in Bilaspur, Sirmaur and Kangra district. Gypsum, bayrites, iron-ore, antimony, asbestos, cobalt, nickel, copper, glass sand and china clay are also found in Himachal, albeit in small quantities, whose exact deposits are yet to be worked out.

TABLE 2.2

Main minerals with their location and reserves

Minerals	Location	Reserves
Limestone	1. Gegal (Bilaspur)	150 m tones (proved)
	2. Boroh (Chamba)	250 m tones (estimated)
	3. Bhadalag (Solan)	52 m tones (estimated)
	4. Dharakot (Kangra)	18.8 m tones (estimated)
	5. Kolhipura (Bilaspur)	20 m tones (estimated)
	6. Kamjota (Bilaspur)	10 m tones (estimated)
	7. Radiana area (Shimla)	0.4 m tones (estimated)
Pyrite	Tara devi (Shimla)	2500 m tones (estimated)
Gypsum	Bhajan & Bharli (Sirmaur)	1 m tones (estimated)

Source: Economic Review of H.P., 1975, Directorate of Economics & Statistics, H.P., Shimla, p. 33.

Population aspects

Growth of population in any environment is of great concern for the resource planners and the situation becomes grave when and where resources are scarce. The growth of population as a consequence of increase in fertility rate and decline of death rate, causes serious threat to the dwindling resources. The mountain environment of Himachal Pradesh does not have very wide resource base, which can cope-up with the increasing population.

The population of Himachal Pradesh has risen from 42.81 lakhs in 1981 to 52.11 lakhs in 1991. The density of population stands at 92 persons per square kilometre, against 267 for the country, which may appear very small but owing to the low carrying capacity of the state, it is fairly high.

Sex ratio

Out of 42,80,818 persons enumerated in 1981 census (51.11 lakh in 1991), 21,69,931 were males and females were 21,10,887 giving the average sex ratio of 973 for the state. In 21 tehsil/sub-tehsils sex ratio is above the parity line while in the remaining 52 units number of females per 1000 males varies between 995 in Nankhari sub-tehsil of Shimla district and 676 in Spiti tehsil of Lahaul and Spiti district. The highest value of sex ratio is found in Lad Bharol (1255) sub-tehsil closely followed by Sandhol (1241) sub-tehsil of Mandi district and Lamba-graon (1207) sub-tehsil of Kangra district. In all tehsils/sub-tehsils of Hamirpur and Sarkaghat tehsil of Mandi, sex ratio fluctuates between 1000-1199 females per 1000 males. Twelve tehsils/sub-tehsils fall in the range of 1000-1099, of which three are located in Kangra and Una, one each in Bilaspur, Solan and Shimla while two are in Kinnaur district. Area containing high values of sex ratio might have experienced the selective outmigration of males in working age-groups to other areas in search of gainful employment.

Unfavourable sex ratio is witnessed in 32 tehsils/sub-tehsils in the range of 900-999 females/1000 males. These tehsils/ sub-tehsils form continuous two distinct regions adjoining the favourable sex ratio area. The first region is located to the south-east of this area extending from Mandi tehsil to Rohru tehsil of Shimla district embracing six tehsils/sub-tehsils of Mandi and Shimla each, three tehsils of Kullu and Sirmaur each, two tehsils/sub-tehsils of Solan and one tehsil of Bilaspur, while the second region is located to the north-west covering south-western Chamba district and Nurpur tehsil and Fatehpur sub-tehsil of Kangra district. The remaining five tehsils/sub-tehsils of the this range are scattered.

The range of 800-899 females/1000 males covers 16 tehsils/ sub-tehsils; out of these units three are located in Sirmaur, Solan and Shimla districts, two in Chamba and one each in Kangra, Lahaul and Spiti, Bilaspur, Kullu and Kinnaur districts. The variation in this range is between 896 in both Nalagarh and Kasauli tehsils of Solan district and 818 in Nichar tehsil of Kinnaur. The last range of below 800 females per 1000 males accounts for the tehsils/sub-tehsils of Spiti (676), Kalpa (749), Shimla (762) and Udaipur (791). The low sex ratio in these areas is caused by migration of male workers engaged in various services, constructions and building of roads, etc.

Literacy rate

The average literacy rate for the state in 1991 is 63.54 per cent. However, highest literacy rate is of Hamirpur (62.7 per cent) followed by Una district (59.78 per cent) and Kangra district (59.37 per cent). The lowest literacy rate is in Chamba district (36.10 per cent). Three districts fall in the range of 49.01-60.00 per cent and covers the districts of Bilaspur, Kangra and Una. Four districts fall in the percentage range of 41.01-55.09 per cent and form a contiguous region, comprising the districts of Kinnaur, Mandi, Solan and Shimla. The fourth range of 33.01-48.09 per cent embraces the districts of Lahaul and Spiti, Sirmaur and Kullu. The area with comparatively higher literacy rate is concentrated in the western part of the state, embracing Kangra, Una, Hamirpur and Bilaspur districts.

Settlement: Urban areas

Lahaul and Spiti and Kinnaur districts are entirely rural. The number of towns in the state stood at 21 in 1901 but this number declined to 11 in 1971 as Nurpur and Kangra (Kangra district), Una (Una district), Nagar and Bhojpur (Mandi district), Bilaspur (Bilaspur district), Rampur (Shimla district), Solan and Nalagarh (Solan district) were declassified. Kasumpti which was a separate town in 1901 (merged with Shimla in 1911). Similarly, Jutogh termed a part of Shimla town in 1911 census. In 1921 census, Bhojpur and Nagar were merged to form a new town, Suket, which was latter renamed as Sundar Nagar in 1931. Since 1921 census the number of urban areas is on constant increase. Their number rose from 12 in 1921 to 19 during 1931, 22 during 1941, 29 in 1951, 30 in 1961, 36 in 1971 and 47 in 1987. The number of places treated as towns increased by 62 per cent between 1951 and 1981. The district-wise distribution of towns as per 1981 census shows that out of the total 47 towns, eight are in Kangra district closely followed by seven in Solan district, six in Shimla, five each in Chamba and Una, four in Mandi, three each in the remaining districts of Hamirpur, Bilaspur, Kullu and Sirmaur districts.

Urban population

The population of urban areas of Himachal has increased to 3,25,971 in 1981 from 77,322 in 1901, thus registering a massive growth during the last 80 years. The urban population has increased more rapidly than the rural areas. The increase is due to the fact that there has been a continuous flow of people from rural to urban areas. The latter having better educational facilities and also larger avenues for employment.

This process of shifting of population from rural to urban areas is found in all the districts of the state.

Only 7.61 per cent of the total population of the state comes from the urban areas and the remaining 92.39 per cent of the population from the rural areas. During the decade 1971-81, the growth of the urban population comes to 34.76 per cent as compared to the general growth rate of 23.71 per cent.

In absolute figures, Shimla districts with urban population of 80,177 ranks first followed by Kangra (48,939), Mandi (47,257) and Solan (32,623). Bilaspur district with a population of 11,585 is at the lowest; whereas Hamirpur district with a population of 15,836 is the second lowest. In terms of percentage, Shimla district shares a proportion of 24.60 per cent of the total urban population of the state followed by Kangra (15.01 per cent) and Mandi (14.50 per cent) while Bilaspur district having only 3.55 per cent of the total urban population of the state is at the bottom, and the share of Hamirpur district comes only to 4.86 per cent.

Rural areas

The village generally follows the limits of a revenue village which is recognised by the district administration. The revenue village need not be a single agglomeration of habitation, but the revenue village has definite surveyed boundaries.

The pattern of a village in hills is somewhat different from plains. The cultivated land is scattered and people live generally in isolated hamlets nearer to their fields. Life and property have been comparatively safe and the necessity for large number of people grouping together in strong collective homesteads had not risen as in the plains.

The term village as used in Himachal during 1981 census denotes village throughout the state except the districts of Kangra, Hamirpur and Kullu and parts of Una and Lahaul and

Spiti districts where 'Tikka' and 'Phatti' have been taken as the rural units.

As per 1981 census total number of villages comes to 18,721 of which 16,807 are inhabited and the remaining 1914 are uninhabited. The uninhabited villages refers to those villages from where no population have been reported although they have their existence in the revenue records. In addition, 143 villages have been fully merged in the urban areas of the state while the number of partly merged villages comes to 114. As per 1981 census, 47 places have been taken as towns in the state as against 36 in 1971. The total number of villages during 1971 census stood at 18,929, of which 16,916 were inhabited and 2013 uninhabited. The decrease in the number of villages may be attributed to the settlement operations in Kangra district. In addition, some of the villages have been fully merged in the urban areas like in Kangra district. Kangra district has the maximum percentage (21.75) of rural population followed by Mandi (17.7) and Solan (13.36) while Kinnaur with one per cent is at the bottom.

There has been a persistent rise in the number of inhabited villages till 1971. The major factor leading to this situation is the increase of the pressure of population on land. As a result of which more and more land was put to agricultural uses and cultivators set-up their own homesteads around the culturable land, which were latter recognised as separate villages. Settlement operations also contributed towards this increase as larger villages were split into smaller villages for the purpose of the collection of land revenue. A slight decline of 109 inhabited villages in 1981 census is due to the settlement operations carried out in Kangra district, where small villages were clubbed for revenue purposes.

As for districts there has been no change in the number of inhabited villages in Kullu and Kinnaur districts during 1971-81. The increase is almost negligible in Chamba, Hamirpur, Lahaul and Spiti and Sirmaur districts. The increase in the number of inhabited villages is of the order of 37 in Shimla, 31 in Bilaspur, 21 in Solan and 17 in Mandi. This increase is due to the reason that certain villages which are uninhabited in 1971 census have recorded population in these areas in 1981 census. The number of uninhabited villages has gone down to 1914 in 1981 as against 2013 in the 1971 census. Kangra and Una are the only districts that have registered a decline in the number of inhabited villages.

Rural population

The distribution of rural population among districts varies to a large extent in 1981 census as also in previous censuses. According to 1981 census Kangra is the most populous with 9,41,820 persons living in rural areas. This is followed by Mandi and Shimla districts. Kangra district, alone accounts for 23.8 per cent of the rural population of the state. The share of rural population in Mandi and Shimla districts is of the order of 15.11 per cent and 10.86 per cent, respectively. The rural population of all other districts is less than the district average of 3,29,571 persons.

Rural population of Chamba, Una, Bilaspur, Mandi and Sirmaur districts shows continuous increase since 1901. It may be seen that till 1951 census the trend in the growth of rural population was rather slow and marked with wide variation among the districts. The increase in population gained momentum only after 1951 census. Improvement in medical facilities and detention of epidemic scourage have their premium to add to this population explosion.

Religion composition

Religion is an important facet of Indian culture. Every decennial census provides an interesting picture of the religious composition of the population inhabiting different parts of the country. Himachal is predominantly inhabited by Hindus while persons professing other religions have got a microscopic strength.

The Hindus constitute 95.77 per cent of the state population. Muslims constitute 1.63 per cent. The Buddhists comprise 52,629 persons closely followed by Sikhs with 52,209 persons, while Christian population comes to only 3954. Merely 1046 persons of Jain community are found in the state. In terms of percentage Buddhists constitute 1.23 per cent of the state population closely followed by Sikhs with 1.22 per cent while Christian and Jains each share a proportion of less than one per cent.

Scheduled castes and Scheduled tribes

There are 1,96,973 Scheduled Caste households in the state of which 1,84,075 are in rural areas and the remaining 12,898 in urban areas.

Among Scheduled Tribes 36,053 households are found in rural areas while in urban areas it is 989 households accounting altogether at state level 37,042 households.

The male and female breakup of Scheduled Castes being 5,37,989 and 5,15,969, while for Scheduled Tribes it is 99,727 and 97,536 respectively.

The percentage-wise comparative study of Scheduled Castes reveal that in 1961 census it was 22.89 per cent of the total population which slightly went down in 1971 with 22.24 per cent. But in 1981 it rose to 24.62 per cent. The spatial analysis says that Scheduled Castes population has registered considerable decline in Mandi district, from 19.40 per cent in 1971 to 10.63 per cent in 1981. The decline, however, was technical in the sense that most of the Scheduled Caste population preferred to declare themselves as Scheduled Tribes rather than Scheduled Castes. Noticeably, they have done so during the 1981 census.

Medical facilities

The number of medical institutions per 10,000 of occupied census houses in the state works out to 16.63. The proportion fluctuates between 14.76 in Kangra district and 32.95 in Lahaul and Spiti district. Number of medical institutions is highest in the north-eastern and eastern parts of the state covering two districts of Kinnaur (27.66) and Lahaul and Spiti which are covered under first range of above 23.00. Second range spreads in the southern and south-western extreme of the state covering districts of Sirmaur (19.29) and Solan (12.95). Third range showing the number of medical institutions between 15.01-19.00 covers six districts of Kullu (15.35), Shimla (15.54), Una (15,71), Bilaspur (16.37), Hamirpur (17.29) and Chamba (18.59). The lowest number of medical institutions is recorded in Kangra (14.28), followed by Mandi (14.82) and both the districts which are covered in the fourth category of below 15.01. In general, it is observed that the areas having lower density of population in the state have higher number of medical institutions per 10,000 occupied census houses, while this number decreases in the areas having higher density of population.

The number of hospital beds/1,00,000 of population in the state is 131.10. The number is highest in Kinnaur district (277.10), followed by Shimla district (240.20). Both these districts are included in the first range of above 220.00, covering the eastern and south-eastern parts of the state. Second range of 160.01-220.00 includes three districts viz. Solan (214.00) Lahaul & Spiti (199.40) and Chamba (169.70). Third range of 100.01-160.00 which also covers state average, includes four districts namely Sirmaur (146.00), Kangra (113.20), Bilaspur (108.70) and Mandi (102.00). The lowest range of below 100.01 covers three districts of Kullu (90.10), Hamirpur (51.00) and Una (33.10).

CHAPTER 3

Levels of Economic Development

There is an increasing awareness now, even among the economists of a neo-classical persuasion that the question of poverty and inequality, or equality in general, are of paramount importance in the context of less developed region. It is instructive to note here that Theodore W. Schultz, in his famous observation notes that: "Most of the people in the world are poor, so if we knew the Economics of being poor we would know much of the Economics that really matters." Taking his cue from Schultz, Gerald M. Meier authored *Emerging from Poverty—The Economics that Really Matters*. All these show that whether one is concerned with defining development, or with form, formulating strategies of development, or else with appraising development performance, the distributional dimension of development has come to the fore.

For purposes of comparison between the two areas here, however, we would classify them as under:

1. 'Old' Himachal—Districts of Bilaspur, Chamba, Kinnaur, Mandi, Shimla and Sirmaur.
2. 'New' Himachal—Districts of Hamirpur, Kangra, Kullu, Lahaul & Spiti and Una.

District Solan has been excluded from both the categories because of its mongrel origin. It may also be noted that the Shimla district contains areas from 'Old' Himachal except the capital town Shimla itself, which belongs to 'new' Himachal Pradesh.

The former accounts for 48.4 per cent of the area and 52.3 per cent of the population, while the latter for the remaining 51.6 per cent of area and 47.7 per cent of the population of the State (excluding Solan district). From the standpoint of comparison of level of development attainment, it is important to keep this difference in area and population in mind because the level of development can be meaningfully appraised only in terms of its human (population) dimension. Sometimes only the human dimension is relevant (e.g. availability of foodgrains per capita), but in some other cases, both human and geographical dimensions are meaningful (e.g. road length per lakh of population and per hundred square kilometres of area).

Available data reflecting on the levels of development of the two segments of the economy have been given in Tables 3.1 and 3.2.

In Table 3.1, change in the intra-regional levels of development of the two areas within a specified period has been compared with each other. In Table 3.2, differences with current levels of development of the two sub-regions in relation to their population and areas have been delineated.

It may be inferred from Table 3.1 that during 1970s, there has been, by and large, greater development in the 'Old' than in the 'new' areas. To be precise, out of the nine indicators taken here, there has been greater development (a higher rate of change) in the 'old' areas in terms of six indicators, but less development in terms of three, and nearly equal development (in farm productivity) in terms of one indicator.

In Table 3.2, the current level of development of the two sub-regions, in relation to their area and population, has been compared. In this table, the comparison has been made in terms of a larger number of indicators because of easier availability of districtwise data for the early 1980. It would be noted in the table that out of eleven indicators taken, the 'old' areas come out to be more developed in terms of seven Indica-

TABLE 3.1

Changes in levels of development of 'old' and 'new' areas

S. No.	Indicators of development	'Old' areas			'New' areas		
		1972-73	1981-82	% change	1972-73	1981-82	% change
		1	2	3	4	5	6
1.	No. of bank branches	41	196	37.80	61	158	159.0
2.	No. of villages electrified	2046	5481	167.9	951	4336	355.9
3.	Net area irrigated ('000 hectares)	38.1	41.1 a	7.8	48.8	41.8 a	(–) 14.3
4.	Literacy ratio (3)	23.3 b	38.0 b	14.7	29.1 b	47.6 b	18.5
5.	No. of colleges	12	13 g	8.3	12 e	12 g	0
6.	No. of students in						
	(a) schools ('000)	285.4 f	405.0 a	41.9	352.6 f	445.9 a	26.5
	(b) colleges	6662 e	10517 g	57.9	4720 c	8834	87.2
7.	No. of regd. factories	91 e	356d	291.2	100 c	355 d	255.0
8.	Road length (km)	5528 f	6940	25.5	4258 f	5143	20.8
9.	Yield (tonne/hectare) of						
	(a) Wheat	1.1	1.3 a	23.8	1.1	1.2 a	13.2
	(b) Maize	1.6	1.8 a	14.6	1.5	1.8 a	19.2
	(c) Rice	0.9	1.2 a	31.9	0.9	1.1 a	22.2

a—Figures for 1980-81; b—Census data; c—Figures for 1971; d—Figures for 1982; e—Figures for 1977-78; f—Figures for 1976-77; g—Figures for 1982-83.

Source: DESHP, Statistical Outline of Himachal Pradesh 1973, 1978, 1980 and 1983; and Directorate of Land Records, H.P., Annual Season and Crop Report for the year 1972-73.

TABLE 3.2

Level of development relatively to area, population, or number of villages: 1981-82

S. No.	Indicator of development	'Old' area	'New' area
1.	No. of school per lakh of population	212 a	160 a
2.	No. of students per lakh of population in		
	(a) Schools	19460 b	23506 b
	(b) Colleges	506	466
3.	No. of bank branches per lakh of population	9	8
4.	Road length per 100 sq. km of area (in km.)	26.7	18.6
5.	Percentage of villages with drinking water facility	54.1	66.0
6.	No. of medical institutions per lakh of population	20.2 c	15.2 c
7.	No. of hospital beds per lakh of population	132.6 c	63.8 c
8.	Per capita availability of foodgrains (in kg.)	238.3 d	213.6 d
9.	Literacy percentage (Census data)	38.0	47.6
10.	No. of registered factories per lakh of population	16	18

a— Figures for calendar year 1982.

b— Figures for 1980-81.

c— Figures relate to the year 1983-84. Population figures for the year have been estimated.

d— Based on three years moving average. These figures are calculated as the average of the districts comprising the two sub-regions.

Source: Calculated from figures in DESHP, Statistical Outline of Himachal Pradesh 1983, and unpublished data made available by State Govt. offices.

indicators, and 'new' areas in terms of three, with one indicator (student-population ratio) showing about even development in both sub-regions. In fact, the conclusions emerging from this table merely confirm what followed from figures in Table 3.1.

Thus, it would be quite right to conclude following facts: (i) during the 1970s, the rate of development has been by and large faster in 'the old' areas in comparison to the 'new' areas, and (ii) the current level of development is also higher in the case of 'old' areas. It is obvious that conclusion (ii) is partly the result of (i), but it may also have been partly controlled by the relative lag in the development of the 'new' areas at the time of their merger with the 'old' areas. However, the latter explanation is not supported much by statistical evidence. If we look at columns (3) and (6) of Table 3.1, we would come to know that in comparison to the pre-existing differences in their levels of development, the gap has arisen more during the 1970s.

Thus, the above analysis shows that a problem of inter-regional equity exists in the State. The pattern of resource allocation can be suitably modified to ensure equitable distribution of the fruits of development between the two sub-regions. This should not be difficult in view of a redeeming feature of the situation noticeable in Table 3.1 that in some cases the difference in the level of development of the two areas is not statistically significant.

Structural variables and levels of development

The term development has various connotations. Hence, its denotation extend to a large number of variables. The consideration of various levels of development in that sense must take stock of different structural variables accounting for development and also their spatial expression for establishing their levels. Resource endowment of a region consisting of significant variables are undertrial, whose note is of utmost importance for consideration of development status of the region. However, in selection certain constraints of resources come before where value consideration of the resource becomes a prerequisite.

Cumulative causation has been an important guiding principle if one considers the case of Himachal Pradesh since its inception. Since the state has been having an agrarian economy, varied structural built-up of this sector is of great significance if the present status of levels is to be understood. Development no doubt, stems from different structures of economy, they for sure, get reflected on human resources. This fact of development projection on human resources also gives rise to a basis of evaluation of levels of development through it. It is not only the structures whose changes may account for evaluation of development levels but the infrastructural changes also go a long way in explaining the changes in levels of development.

The present study takes account of resource endowment and economic structural development of different sectors over time to establish spatial variations expressed through administrative units, i.e. districts.

The Himachal economy is largely dependent on primary activities as the industrial base is relatively weak. Further, the primary production to a large extent is still dependent on natural factors like rainfall and weather conditions.

Thus one comes across a primitive economic system with little infrastructural and institutional development while considering economic development at the time of emergence of Himachal from its feudal past. Various sectors of development need to be evaluated while taking stock of the early economic structure.

Early economic development structure

For the purpose of analysis of early economic structure of Himachal Pradesh the most significant questions pertain to the nature of the structure of domestic product of the state and the pattern of utilization of the labour force at that time. The composition of domestic product and varied utilization of labour force for the year 1950-51 has been taken as the base year for explanation in Table 3.3.

TABLE 3.3

The structure of state domestic product and pattern of labour utilisation: 1950-51

Sector	Share in			
	Net state domestic product		Labour force (workers)	
	Rs. in lakhs	% of the total	'000	% to total
Agriculture	1663.43	69.43	587	91.0
Industry	415.32	17.33	42	6.5
Services	317.14	13.24	16	2.5
Total:	2395.89	100.00	645	100.00

Source: Directorate of Economics and Statistics.

During this period the production structure of the state was highly unbalanced. However, it gives some respite if one considers it in relation to the national production structure. As against agriculture with 69.4 per cent, industry, and service contribute 17.3 and 13.2 per cent, respectively, to the State Domestic Product of Himachal Pradesh. The comparative national shares were, however, 51.3, 33.11 and 15.8 per cent, respectively. The structure of domestic product and labour utilisation also highlighted the fact that the economy was suffering from a severe fundamental imbalance.

The structural imbalance in the economy is the outcome of the predominance of the working population in the agricultural sector, as against about one-tenth employed outside it.

This also speaks for the structural rigidity of the economy. The sectors which could record higher productivity were not attracting labour from the low productivity sector due to the poor infrastructural base.

Early human resource structure

The economic development is expressed through human development in quantitative terms. Two major sub-structures of human development are of great significance for understanding the economic development viz. literacy and health facilities.

The quality of human resource could be judged by its literacy level. In the first half of this century Himachal Pradesh had lamentable position in this regard. Only 7.5 per cent of the male and 2.0 per cent of the female population were literate (1951 census). This literacy percentage works out to be 4.8 per cent. It is to be noted that this percentage was the lowest among all the states and union territories of India. The situation of higher skilled and educated population level was more serious which accrue from Table 3.4.

TABLE 3.4

Degree and diploma held in Himachal Pradesh

Nature of degree/diploma held	Number of persons
Art and science graduates	369
Postgraduates of art & science	85
Teachers	338
Medicine	69
Others	1098
Total holders	1959
Percentage of total population	0.18

The situation was the outcome of the poor education infrastructure in the state (Table 3.5). The ratio of educational institutions was one of the poorest in the nation, i.e. one school in an area of about 70 square kilometres inhabited by 2,700 persons in 1948.

TABLE 3.5

Schools in Himachal Pradesh

Level of schools	For boys	For girls	Total
High schools	15	2	17
Middle and lower-middle schools	48	6	54
Primary Schools	328	9	337

The first degree college came about only after Independence and the first industrial training institute is less than three decades old. The state of education, literacy, and skill formation, and also the institutional facilities, speaks of an utter neglect of an important catalytic force, generating conditions for modern economic development.

As far as the health facilities, another significant reflector of human resource development of economic development is concerned, the situation of the first decade of Independence was far from satisfactory. There were 88 hospitals and dispensaries with 209 beds for patients (1948). This made availability of one hospital bed for per 2500 persons. The low population/hospital ratio was also grossly underutilised as the transportation to cities at that time was highly underdeveloped.

Early transportation structure

Movement of goods and services are taken to be prerequisite for development. The construction of road was taken at war level after independence, considering the nature of topography which did not allow any other mode to be developed and also the existing low density of roads at that time. At the time of Independence there existed only 720 kilometres of roads of which only 5.1 per cent was metalled and 25.4 per cent was un-metalled and remaining 69.4 per cent as mule path. The situation appears much more worse if one considers remoteness of population, as there existed only 8 kilometres of surfaced road per lakh of population. As a consequence there existed one of the smallest ratio of vehicles per head in the country. As far as different modes of transportation like air and water are concerned they were completely absent and even the part of the track of two railway lines constructed by the British, that passed through the territory of the then existing Himachal Pradesh, was merely 34 miles.

Early power generation

The use of energy has been adopted by various social scientists to measure economic development. The consideration of great potential of hydroelectricity generation and their realisation in the early eras of planned development, present a picture which clearly explains the low level of economic development in the state. There was a total installed capacity and industrial consumption of electrical power at 503 Kwh and 141 horse power, respectively (1947). The electricity generation capacity was grossly underutilised as the industrial base was far from competent. There were only 20 per cent of the princely capital towns which could boast of electrification. The per capita consumption of electricity in 1948 in the state stood at less than 1 Kwh while the average Indian enjoyed about 18 Kwh.

The near absence of infrastructural facilities, coupled with non-conducive socio-economic structure to modern development, provide ample evidence that Himachal Pradesh must have been a sort of a mosaic of highly retarded sub-economies, with hardly anything to integrate it with the economy of the rest of the country. After the amalgamation of these retarded sub-economies this state was decidedly among the poorest administrative units of India (Sharma 1987). The National Council of Applied Economic Research (NCAER) during sixties identified Himachal Pradesh to be one of the poorest and backward territories in the Indian Union. According to an estimate, in the mid-1950s (1955-56), only three states and union territories in the country, viz., Bihar, Orissa, and Manipur had a per capita income lower than that of Himachal Pradesh (Bose '62). Even those areas which were later merged with this State in 1966 had suffered a similar fate in the pre-independence period. According to the NCAER, these areas, viz., Kangra, Lahaul and Spiti and Shimla, were among the poorest constituents of the composite Punjab in 1955-56, in terms of per capita income (NCAER).

The foregoing discussion on the state of development of the infrastructural facilities, as of late 1940s or early 1950s, would help in putting the nature of the region's initial socio-economic structure into proper focus, since these facilities go long way in shaping the structure of the economy, especially in the initial stages of its development.

Present levels of economic development

Spatio-temporal analysis of economic development

Considering the fact that Himachal Pradesh which was near to bottom position during early planning period, has recorded among first five states at the inception of Eighth Five Year Plan. The phenomenal growth of economy calls for some explanation. Two major hypotheses can be extended in this regard viz., growth of agricultural productivity and relatively egalitarian socio-economic structure (Sharma '87). The low gross agricultural annual out-put per acre in early sixties rose to 2.87 per cent compared to that of the early seventies. Continuing the trend it recorded among first ten states in early eighties. The rural economy of Himachal Pradesh also recorded less incidence of absolute poverty. The poverty ratio of Himachal Pradesh during 1985-90 has been about 2.5 per cent while the corresponding figure for the country was about 50 per cent. Thus, the hypotheses that the houses which have less people below poverty line shall have larger percentage of people participating in developmental activities accelerating the economic development. This was the case with Himachal Pradesh which recorded faster economic growth than most of the other states of the country.

Growth of economy over time can better be understood in reference to different structural indicators which can be used for explaining levels of development with their spatial expression. This is a sort of measure of levels of economic development through growth potential rather than realised growth.

Various economic structural variables as growth indicators

Growth performance of economy can latter be analysed through different economic indicators. The consideration of indicators are important in a variety of ways, as they provide an insight into the growth of an economy in terms of structural variables which otherwise remains concealed in an aggregate analysis. Besides, some of these indicators directly reflect changes taking place in the welfare of the people (such as growth of literacy and education, and public health facilities), which is the aim of economic development. Much more importantly, these indicators act as proxy variables representing the extent of generation of external economies of growth impulses, and thus provide an insight into the potential for future growth that might be getting built into the economy (Sharma '87).

Literacy

Literacy of Himachal Pradesh which was below national average recorded slow growth initially but later in 1951 onwards recorded continuous growth which is shown in Table 3.6. Presently more than half of the population is literate (Table 3.7). During 1961-71 the literacy ratio of Himachal Pradesh rose up by nearly 85 per cent, which was the highest growth

TABLE 3.6

Literacy level

Census year	Literacy percentage	
	Himachal Pradesh	All India
1951	7.7	16.6
1961	21.2	24.0
1971	31.9	29.5
1981	42.5	36.2
1991	63.3	52.2

rate recorded during the period by any state in India (Singh '71). The reason behind this phenomenal increase was partly boosted by the merger of those areas of Punjab, which were having high literacy rate with Himachal Pradesh.

Although Himachal appears to have fared well in this significant indicator over time if we compare with that of the rest of the country. The state shows poor performance in its hill parts in comparison to the plain part of the adjoining plain

TABLE 3.7

Literacy rate change

Districts	Literacy rate	
	1981	1991
Bilaspur	44.69	56.11
Chamba	26.45	36.11
Hamirpur	52.70	62.77
Kangra	49.12	59.37
Kinnaur	36.84	49.39
Kullu	33.82	45.15
Lahaul-Spiti	31.35	48.02
Mandi	40.21	52.20
Shimla	42.74	55.09
Sirmaur	31.78	42.11
Solan	41.07	53.18
Una	50.05	59.78

land. Thus disparity exists over space which could be gauged in Table 3.7.

The literacy rate in Himachal was 63.54 during 1991 census. But this does give hardly any reason to rejoice for male/female literacy differential were wide in the state. Against 74.78 per cent male literacy, the female literacy rate accounted 53.46 per cent. During 1990-91 without taking any expansion activity in elementary, secondary or higher education, intensification was stressed on working of primary schools within a radius of one to one and a half kilometres under the "operation Black Board" scheme. Under the scheme 6,942 primary schools were covered. This project provides teaching and learning material and also additional rooms and teacher facility at grass root level.

So far, technical education is concerned, there are four polytechnics, one junior technical school which has now been upgraded to polytechnic grade, 17 industrial training institutes, including one exclusively meant for physically handicapped. There are 15 industrial training institutes where women are trained exclusively. Post-diploma courses in computer were started in government polytechnic Hamirpur and government Polytechnic for women at Kandaghat in January 1990. In I.T.Is., training in engineering and non-engineering trades is imparted. Since 1986-87, a regional engineering college at Hamirpur is functioning.

Urbanisation

The evaluation of a long-term development performance of an economy could be done by studying the structural change which takes place. It is common to identify development in both the ex-post and ex-ante senses with structural shifts, especially changes in the composition of output (Kingsle Leaser '77). The study of the characteristics of emerging socio-economic structure directly aims at bringing to light, the qualitative changes that might have taken place in an economy

(Chaudhury and Morises '75). Input-output economics, which provides the necessary tools for the study of the structure of an economy, looks at under-development as a manifestation of "incomplete" economic structures (Census of 63). Thus, it is implied that with the process of development, the socio-economic structure becomes more and more perfect, balanced and resilient (Sharma '87).

The change in the production structure brings out mainly the facts about responsiveness of economic system and shift of production function towards better productive sectors. The structural indicators explaining levels could be picked out which studies inter sectoral changes and secondly those which explain intra-sectoral changes. The spatial analysis, the geographical plan of appraisal broadly focus on intra-structural changes for establishing levels of development but the exercise may provide erroneous result if the consideration of intra-sectoral changes like shift towards urbanisation (which has spatial expression) is not considered.

The urban population is on the increase since Independence. It constituted 19.91 per cent, 23.24 per cent and 25.72 per cent during 1971, 1981 and 1991 censuses, respectively. But in the case of Himachal, it has been among the tailenders, since state constituted an urban population percentage of 6.99, 7.61 and 8.70 during the last census years, respectively. The urban population increase worked out to be 1.09 per cent during last decade. However, three districts, namely, Shimla, Solan and Sirmaur have urban population percentage of 20.43, 12.47 and 10.05, respectively (DESHP '92).

This spatio-temporal dimension of urbanization suggests that Himachal has been a state running on farmland which has not seen the level of structural transformation and change in production structure in the last three decades, which the national economy has experienced.

Still, the rate of structural transformation has been quite fast to ensure the ongoing shift of resources away from agriculture to industry and service sectors. The other facet of economic transformation in terms of production structure, it is not wise to compare with that of the nation for it grows and gets transformed according to their resource endowments and their development momentum within state at sub-economy level should be appraised (Table 3.8).

TABLE 3.8

Urbanization in Himachal Pradesh

Districts	Percent urban population		% change
	1981	1991	
Bilaspur	4.6	5.7	23.91
Chamba	6.8	7.6	11.76
Hamirpur	4.9	6.3	28.57
Kangra	4.9	4.8	–2.0
Kinnaur	100	100	0
Kullu	7.0	7.0	0
Lahaul-Spiti	100	100	0
Mandi	7.3	7.2	–1.36
Shimla	15.6	20.4	30.76
Sirmaur	8.7	10	14.94
Solan	10.7	12.4	15.88
Una	7.7	8.6	11.68

Agriculture

The intra-sectoral qualitative change has widely been accepted as an important tool for evaluating the levels of development. Agriculture, being the single most important sector of the state, has been evaluated here, in terms of its qualitative changes. Various parameters of this sector when evaluated at district level will provide clue to the changes in their sub-economy operating at spatial context.

In Himachal Pradesh, the total output as well as the total labour force in agriculture sector has shown decline. However, this does not imply the decadence of this sector in terms of total sectoral output, productivity and other qualitative characteristics. It is to be noted here that while the relative importance of the agricultural sector had been declining, perceptible qualitative intra-sectoral changes had been taking place at the same time (Sharma '87). The changes within this sector at district level in terms of crop production, input, livestock, etc. may be evaluated which again have fairly reliable economic expression.

The production structure of food and non-food crops, if analysed in the context of time and space, provide expression that significant changes have taken place particularly in terms of non-food crops during 1985-90. The change explains very well the demand of land in other economic activities which sometimes is also higher foodgrain requirement. The stress on commercial fruits, apple, has shown that it is one of the great fluctuating crops of the state and explains the presence and role of variety of factors that may bring about drastic change in its total production. Export figure of apple has been used as an indicator of growth of production as it is mainly a commercial crop grown for consumption outside the production region (Table 3.9). The need is to make this crop less variable to enhance dependability of the growers on it.

TABLE 3.9

Apple export 1985-90 in selected districts of Himachal Pradesh

Districts	Export of apples in tonnes			
	1985	1986	1987	1988
Shimla	70075	190692	137218	84141
Kullu	48189	67141	55229	30920
Mandi	9483	13616	5477	6301
Kinnaur	7831	8852	5861	8063
Chamba	2975	5141	2973	1892
Solan	140	17	84	81
Sirmaur	960	1786	517	702
Kangra	21	25	43	39
Lahaul-Spiti	20	34	19	13

Intra-sectoral change is better explained through the level of development expressed if one considers the adoption of modern input package variation amongst different units. The use of high yielding variety is one indicator which explains the development made by agriculture in the unit area under consideration in Tables 3.10 and 3.11.

TABLE 3.10

Food & non-food production

(in tonnes)

	Food crop (G.C.A.)		Non-food crop (G.C.A)		% change (1985-90)	
	1985	1990	1985	1990	Food crop	Non-food crop
Bilaspur	59444	59720	1187	1191	0.46	0.33
Chamba	60919	61923	2744	2402	1.64	(–) 12.46
Hamirpur	74571	73579	292	294	(–) 1.33	2.39
Kangra	208741	203402	15831	14328	(–) 2.55	(–) 9.49
Kinnaur	9742	9382	33	45	(-) 3.69	36.36
Kullu	56937	57947	1446	788	1.59	(–) 45.50
Lahaul-Spiti	3004	3125	301	126	4.02	(–) 58.13
Mandi	150804	157676	2193	2295	4.55	4.65
Shimla	110025	107937	581	552	(–) 1.89	(–) 4.99
Sirmaur	76070	74428	3103	3214	(–) 2.15	3.57
Solan	66966	66525	3550	3281	(–) 0.65	(–) 7.57
Una	70487	74415	4117	4356	5.57	5.80

The differential productivity growth has led to the reallocation of farm land in favour of those crops which have shown highest productivity growth, that is, wheat in most districts of the State. Modern input such as fertilizer (nitrogen, phosphorous and potassium) is also found to be concentrating in agriculturally developed districts (Table 3.12).

Himachal Pradesh whose different rivers supply water to the fields of agriculturally developed states like Punjab and Haryana is not being used for its own due to the topographical reasons. Kuhls by far have remained the most important source of irrigation in the state. Himachal Pradesh as a whole still

TABLE 3.11

Area under high-yielding variety crops

(in thousand hectares)

	Wheat	% of total wheat prod-ucing area	Paddy	% of the total	Maize	% of the total	Net area 1 + 3 + 5	% of HYV wheat area in the dist.	% of HYV paddy area in the dist.	% of HYV maize area in the dist.
	1	2	3	4	5	6	7	8	9	10
Bilaspur	26.00	7.73	3.60	3.80	10.00	10.00	39.60	65.60	9.00	25.00
Chamba	18.00	5.34	3.20	3.30	7.00	7.00	28.20	63.80	11.30	24.80
Hamirpur	30.00	3.90	3.10	3.20	12.00	12.00	45.10	66.50	6.80	26.60
Kangra	82.00	24.33	30.25	32.00	13.00	13.00	125.25	65.40	24.10	10.30
Kinnaur	1.50	0.45	–	–	–	–	1.50	100.00	–	–
Kullu	19.00	5.63	2.60	2.70	7.00	7.00	28.60	66.40	9.90	24.40
Lahaul-Spiti	–	0	–	–	–	–	–	–	–	–
Mandi	58.50	17.30	29.50	31.20	23.50	23.50	111.50	52.40	26.40	21.00
Shimla	28.00	8.30	7.60	8.00	4.50	4.50	40.10	69.80	18.90	11.20
Sirmaur	29.00	8.60	4.30	4.50	8.00	8.00	41.30	70.20	10.40	19.30
Solan	25.00	7.40	4.10	4.30	10.00	10.00	39.10	63.90	10.40	22.50
Una	20.00	5.90	3.00	3.10	5.00	5.00	28.00	77.40	10.70	17.80
Total	337.00		91.25		100.00		528.25			

TABLE 3.12

Fertilizer (NPK)* consumption in different districts

(in tonnes)

Districts	1987-88	1989-90
Bilaspur	1550	2222
Chamba	609	732
Hamirpur	1755	2603
Kangra	4534	6596
Kinnaur	108	149
Kullu	1506	2147
Lahaul-Spiti	386	381
Mandi	3775	4591
Shimla	4799	5242
Sirmaur	1354	1867
Solan	1950	2523
Una	3019	3658

*NPK = Nitrogen, phosphorus and potassium.

ranks amongst one of the tailenders as far as irrigation is concerned. The diversities of irrigation sources are very low and have rather been static over time across districts (Table 3.13). It is irrigation's lack which also explains the low consumption of other modern input of agriculture like high yielding varieties of seed and chemical fertilizers. Despite these impediments within national perspective the state has not done so badly and in fact the productivity growth of agriculture has been fairly high.

The intra-sectoral analysis of agriculture, the only significant sector of economy indicates that despite the fact that certain sectors have recorded growth like high-yielding variety adoption and fertilizer use it is not uniform across the state. This may be explained by differential geographical factors, consequent upon population distribution. One factor which has dampened the situation and acts as a great drag to agricultural development is lack of irrigation. The high input by the farmer is often avoided in the wake of uncertainty that pre-

TABLE 3.13

Various sources of irrigation

(in hectares)

	Canal			Well & Tubewell			Tank			Kuhls & other sources		
District	1986-87	87-88	88-89	1986-87	87-88	88-89	1986-87	87-88	88-89	1986-87	87-88	88-89
Bilaspur	271	569	569	564	213	192	22	–	–	2052	3528	3549
Chamba	–	–	–	–	–	–	–	–	–	3590	3513	3550
Hamirpur	–	–	–	52	10	108	–	41	–	1729	1715	1658
Kangra	–	–	–	184	184	1616	–	–	–	32327	32327	30895
Kinnaur	–	–	–	–	–	–	–	–	–	3435	4373	4259
Kullu	–	–	–	–	–	13	–	–	–	2224	2105	2230
Lahaul-Spiti	–	–	–	–	–	–	–	–	–	3105	3092	3161
Mandi	–	–	–	176	302	633	–	–	–	13214	13331	13340
Shimla	–	–	–	–	–	–	–	–	–	4875	4875	4624
Sirmaur	3694	3818	3774	1801	1840	3058	14	15	–	8057	8017	8086
Solan	2577	2315	2132	967	1126	2586	567	515	–	6045	504	5124
Una	47	–	–	–	2937	3894	–	–	–	3874	1461	1464

vails within the rain-fed irrigation system.

Different resources for economic development

Human capital resources

The dual nature of human kind as both the means and end of developmental strategies has always baffled social scientists about its treatment. However, a general unanimity exists as far as quality improvement is concerned for treating it to be a reserve base for larger development in broader framework. The qualitative changes that come about in it, have variety of expressions whose measuring tools are also varied. Mehta ('76) and Harbinson-Myers have been the champion in their approach, wherein they ranked the countries of the world according to the human resource development. The exact indices they used for such purpose included the number of teachers, engineers, scientists, physicians and dualist. Keeping in view the difference in economic built-up of the Himachal sub-economy a different set of indices are proposed to be used. The indices which are observed to explain the level of human capital resource at district level include literacy rate, per cent of workers to total population and per cent of S.C./S.T. students reaching up to class IX-XII to the corresponding registered in class I-V. As far as the statistics suggest Shimla averages as a district which is the best of the lot if human capital accumulation is accounted for. It is followed by Solan and Kangra, very closely.

If compared amongst themselves they give interesting results. All variables appear highly exclusive and represent different dimensions of human stock. Their mutual exclusiveness explains their position from more than one dimension. The high rate of education does not entail Hamirpur to bring forth the S.C./S.T. students into the mainstream and there they fall at a position which is lowest among the districts. The absolute consideration of S.C./S.T. figures have been rising as some districts which absorbed them may have pulled result to their side and a relative per cent figure of enrolment and passing out class V-XII has been considered.

The population of Himachal Pradesh has risen from 42.81 lakhs according to 1981 census to 51.11 lakhs in 1991. The change in quality of population resource is of greater significance than the change in number. The density of Himachal which stands at 92 persons/kilometre square against 267 for the country may appear very small but owing to its low carrying capacity it is fairly high and the rate of population has been 19.39 per cent which is better than the national growth rate (23.5 per cent). The sex ratio has been continuously increasing in the state since the beginning of this century from 884 (1901) to 996 (1991) against all-India level of 972 (1901) which dipped further to 929 (1991).

Development of Scheduled tribes and Scheduled castes

An indepth review of the tribal situation on the eve of the Eighth Plan revealed that the scheduled tribes by and large continued to remain socially and economically backward. Hence, the concept of tribal sub-plan was conceived for accelerated socio-economic development of tribal areas. The tribal sub-plan strategy comprised identification of development of tribal areas. The tribal sub-plan strategy comprised identification of development blocks having 50 per cent or more scheduled tribes population, earmarking funds for the tribal sub-plan from the Central and State plan sectoral outlays; and financial institutions; and supplementation from the Central pool of special central assistance, creation of appropriate administrative structures in tribal areas and adoption of appropriate personnel policies. The tribal areas in the State are the districts of Kinnaur, Lahaul & Spiti and Pangi and Bharmaur tehsils and sub-tehsil Holi of Chamba district. During the Sixth Plan, Modified Area Development Approach (MADA) was devised to cover the dispensed scheduled tribes population under sub-plan treatment and two pockets of tribal concentration, viz. Chamba and Bhattiyat were identified. In the Sixth Plan, emphasis also shifted from welfare to family and beneficiary oriented development schemes within the general programmes. Together with tribal areas, 63 per cent of the scheduled tribes population was covered under sub-plan treatment. For the Eighth Plan, these basic premises continue to hold good. The State Plan flow to the Tribal Sub-Plan has been 8.62 per cent for the Sixth Plan and 9 per cent for the Seventh Plan against which the actual achievement had been 8.78 per cent. In the annual plans 1990-91 and 1991-92 such flow was of the order of 9.95 per cent and 9 per cent, respectively. During 1991-92, in the annual state plan size of Rs. 36.90 crores and Special Central Assistance Supplementation was Rs. 3.45 crores. The Special Central Assistance received for the tribal pockets was Rs. 0.121 crores. The highest priority was accorded to the Economic Services Sector. The scheduled tribes outside the tribal areas and tribal pockets were brought under the sub-plan treatment for the first time in 1987-88 when Special Central Assistance benefit was extended to them that received Rs. 0.17 crores for 1991-92 (DESHP '90).

Infrastructural development

Infrastructure development is the prerequisite on which the edifice of development can be built. Investment in economic infrastructure yields directly very small interest in income. It creates, however, a framework necessary to the profitableness of more immediately lucrative subsequent investments (Rodan '69). Infrastructure facilities are better studied in relative form, i.e. its availability per unit area or population. Keeping in view the anthropogenic and geographical condition of Himachal certain infrastructural facilities gain importance in performance over others. The facilities of greater significance, include transport and communication, health, income and commercial institution like banking, etc.

Transportation and communication

Movement of goods and services are both prerequisite and catalyst of development. Owing to hilly nature of state and low density of population and high maintenance cost, transportation development was not given due importance till Seventh Plan since it started to a more respectable position in four decades of development which is obvious in Table 3.14.

TABLE 3.14

Roads

Year	Motorable road	Roads per sq. kms. of area	Roads per 1000 of population
1950-51	352	1.25	3.17
1955-56	718	2.57	6.14
1960-61	1,443	5.16	10.83
1965-66	2,137	7.58	12.78
1966-67	4,221	7.58	13.40
1970-71	7,609	13.67	22.22
1975-76	10,189	18.30	26.82
1978-79	11,402	20.47	28.36
1979-80	11,993	21.53	29.25
1980-81	12,605	22.63	30.16
1981-82	13,123	23.56	30.81
1982-83	13,600	24.43	31.41
1983-84	14,025	25.19	31.80
1990-91	16,883	30.32	23.03

Economic and social development depends a lot on efficient system of communication. Roads are the lifeline of the state for practically no other means of communication are at their disposal. Which is why high priority has been accorded to the road construction programmes. Definitely this mountain region gives no option but to depend solely on roads.

Before planning era Himachal did not attract rulers of the different princely states to develop efficient communication between their states. The Britishers, on the other hand connected only hill stations with plain and some effort was made in laying of railway lines between Kalka and Shimla and between Pathankot and Joginder Nagar. It did not attract further attention owing to heavy cost of building and maintenance. As a consequence large areas remained unconnected— travelling for which was both strenuous as well as hazardous.

The planning period after independence was the period of realisation of significance of road construction. And for the purpose nearly one-third of the Plan outlay was spent on road construction.

Further watershed in road construction in Himachal Pradesh comes when areas of Punjab were integrated with it to form greater Himachal Pradesh (1966). Despite the fact that the area of the state was nearly doubled the addition of roads did not keep in that proportion.

There are various impediments in road construction and chief being the topographical variation, new age of mountain and to top it all criss-crossing perennial streams. The history of road-bridge construction for heavy traffic is only three decades old. The major bridge which connects vital remote areas of state include bridge of river Yamuna at Paonta Sahab connecting Himachal Pradesh with Uttar Pradesh, the bridge at Nadavn on river Beas which connects Shimla with Bilaspur and Dharamshala with Chamba. The bridges over river Sutlej include Kadror, Slapper, Tattapani, Luri, Nogli, Kharo, Moorang and Gyumthing. River Ravi has many suspension bridges like the one at Bagga, Chaurah and Sitla. It shows that large number of bridges have been constructed and many more are under construction, indicating that Himachal Pradesh is progressing very fast in the field of road construction.

The construction of roads has made a significant impact on the economy of the Pradesh. The proverbial inaccessible areas of Lahaul and Spiti and Kinnaur, outer areas of Kullu district, Pachhad and Rainka tehsils of Sirmaur district, Janjheli area of Mandi district and Brahmaur and Tissa areas of Chamba district have been connected with motorable roads. Much amenities have not been provided so far, but this problem will be tackled as soon as some headway is made in comparatively less difficult areas (Mian Goverdhan Singh).

There have been various facilities which have accrued due to growth in road density, such as the transportation of essential goods, exploitation of agroclimatic resources, horticulture, etc. in the form of development. Another facet of advantage associated with road construction is that it also provides employment to more than 50,000 persons every year. The extension of electricity was made possible to remote areas only after they were connected with roads as connection of electricity involves also transportation of lines and transformers to newer areas.

The spatial distribution of the level of this infrastructure development has been uniform owing to several historical and geographical factors (Table 3.15). The road density speaks of the economic built-up of the region and also the movement of things as essential prerequisite of development. There has been general increase in road density in all the districts of Himachal Pradesh except Chamba where decline has been noted mainly contributed by the decline of 26.7 per cent in unmetalled roads despite the fact that metalled road has increased (10.75 per cent).

The comparison between the figures of the state and that of the nation, in respect of road kilometres per lakh population during 1978-79, the state of Himachal boasted having double of the national figure. However, when considered per hundred square kilometres of area, the road length of the former was only 88 per cent of that of the latter (DESHP '83). It is an interesting character of Himachal in terms of infrastructural development while it has made impressive strides in the development of infrastructural facilities which still remain in-

TABLE 3.15

Road density

(in sq. kms.)

Districts	1985-86	1989-90
Bilaspur	79	79
Chamba	16	15
Hamirpur	77	82
Kangra	50	56
Kinnaur	06	07
Kullu	12	14
Lahaul-Spiti	03	05
Mandi	50	59
Shimla	42	44
Sirmaur	52	55
Solan	61	63
Una	61	74

adequate in relation to its population and the geographical expansion. This is a dilemma of hill area development ingrained in the low density of population which is hard to resolve (Sharma '87).

The factors like low density of population (less than 5 persons per square kilometre) and very high cost of construction of roads account for a great deal of diversity between road development and consequently the development of means of transportation in the remote areas of the state.

The length of railway routes in Himachal Pradesh was at 209 kilometres in 1991. There are only two narrow gauge railway lines connecting Shimla with Kalka (96 kilometres) and Jogindernagar with Pathankot (113 kilometres). During 1990-91 Himachal Pradesh has been brought on the broad gauge map of the Indian Railways in January 1991 with the commissioning of the 16 kilometres Nangal Dam-Una railways.

During eighties there was only one airstrip in Himachal Pradesh i.e., at Bhuntar in Kully valley. A constant need was felt by planners to boost tourism and to break the remoteness of hill stations. During Seventh Plan period two airports namely Shimla at Jubbar-Hati and Kangra at Gaggal were taken in hand and made operational with a view to boost tourism in the Pradesh. The Shimla airport was made operational in May 1987 and Kangra airport in May 1990. With construction of the airports, Kangra and Shimla valleys have been connected by air with the rest of the country. Presently the helipads are available at Dodra Kawar, Kaza, Keylong, Killar, Rohru, Bankuffar, Tabo, Mandi, Chharabra, Rampur and Dharampur and the construction work of helipad at Chamba is in progress and is likely to be completed soon.

Communication development is very significant infrastructure whose pressure and level of development usher in several other developmental factors. The number of post offices in the state was only 314 in 1956 which rose to more than two thousand in eighties but the per thousand availability rose from 2.68 post offices per ten thousand population to less than six per ten thousand population in the corresponding period. This fact is explained by the growth in the population what this region recorded after independence.

Thus when considered in relation to the growth of population, the growth of means of communications has been rather inadequate in the state. This impression is reinforced by the fact that in 1982, there were only 33 telephones per 10,000 of population in the State. The low density of population in the hills renders the task of providing public goods like telephones and postal facilities difficult, but the dispersed nature of population also provides the *raison d'etra* for more communication facilities (Sharma '87).

Power generation

Power Generation and consumption of energy has been a very significant indicator for establishing the levels of development. Despite the fact that the region is having vast potentiality of hydroelectricity it had to face transmission problem and bias consumption rate due to low industrialisation, initially. Since Independence about 300 per cent growth in generation has been recorded while the per capita increase in consumption has been to the tune of nearly ten per cent. The region which used to be deficit in electricity has become an electricity surplus store supplying to nearby states, since early eighties. As far as spatial distribution of this economic growth habit is concerned the state preserves a rather uniform situation which is obvious from Table 3.16.

TABLE 3.16

Electrification

Districts	No. of inhabited villages	Villages electrified 1985	Villages electrified 1988
Bilaspur	911	857	911
Chamba	1095	902	1084
Hamirpur	1619	1526	1619
Kangra	3974	3681	3974
Kinnaur	77	72	77
Kullu	169	132	169
Lahaul-Spiti	235	153	235
Mandi	2789	2116	2789
Shimla	2188	2044	2188
Sirmaur	965	867	965
Solan	2337	1789	2337
Una	557	475	557
	16916*		16778*

Source: DESHP.

*The difference of 138 villages was due to the fact that 118 villages emerged and rest 20 villages which were electrified were uninhabited villages by March 1988.

Commercial banking

Commercial banking is an important catalyst and indicator of development and factor for distribution of development.

The banking situation like economic status, was at its worst before the independence. The growth of banking in Himachal Pradesh was slow initially and fast after the formation of greater Himachal Pradesh as well as after bank nationalisation. The low density of population, its poor economy and less developed transportation calls for a situation where there are larger number of banks available per lakh of population.

As far as the recent scenario in commercial banking is concerned it has recorded 2.4 per cent growth in number of establishment during 1990 and 1991. The spatial level of development of this growth habit clearly shows that it is in keeping with the advancement of allied growth habit of economy and has recorded highest in Kangra (129.9) followed by Shimla (15.5 per cent). The rural orientation of economy can also be better understood as 89 per cent of the total banks are located in rural areas (1991). The spatial distribution which speaks for the level of development in commercial activities is not uniform in Himachal Pradesh as certain districts like Kangra and Shimla which have higher number of banks do not fare well when compared with the availability of banks per ten thousand of population (Table 3.17). Kangra district which has highest number of banks also records second highest in total deposit but its per capita deposit is one of the lowest.

Medical facilities

In a welfare state like India the ultimate aim of economic development is the betterment of the citizens. The infrastructural facilities such as medical facilities is of great significance as far as agrarian economy is concerned.

The figures for 1966, given in Table 3.18 are not very reliable, for this being the year of reorganisation of the state. However, the medical facilities are studied in the following table in relation to the number of hospitals, dispensaries, medical and public health facilities, doctors and availability of hospital beds (Table 3.18).

TABLE 3.17

Commercial banking (1989)

Districts	No. of banks	Per ten thousand population		
		No. of banks	Deposit	Credit
Bilaspur	37	1.20	127.9	36.9
Chamba	53	1.30	113.5	35.9
Hamirpur	47	1.30	281.4	42.6
Kangra	138	1.20	23.8	49.2
Kinnaur	16	2.30	118.2	49.2
Kullu	43	14.30	20.2	73.4
Lahaul-Spiti	6	1.90	206.0	40.2
Mandi	86	1.10	142.7	151.7
Shimla	111	1.80	441.2	155.4
Sirmaur	42	1.10	103.1	7.1
Solan	69	1.80	246.3	239.6
Una	40	1.10	248.3	76.2

TABLE 3.18

Growth of medical and health facilities

Year	Hospitals and dispensaries		Doctors and vaids		Hospital beds available	
	No.	No. per 10,000 of population	No.	No. per 10,000 of population	No.	No. per 10,000 of population
1	2	3	4	5	6	7
1950-51	91	0.82	85	0.77	455	4.10
1955-56	164	1.40	230	1.97	988	8.44
1960-61	225	1.69	228	1.71	1348	10.12
1965	266	1.59	274	1.64	1992	11.91
1966	480	1.52	688	2.18	4649	14.76
1970	587	1.71	639	1.87	4531	13.23
1975	692	1.82	731	1.92	5224	13.75
1980	738	1.76	1074	2.57	5588	13.37
1981	741	1.74	1163	2.74	5622	13.23
1982	806	1.87	1232	2.87	5715	13.29
1983	831	1.88	–	–	5974	13.55
1989	926	1.81	–	–	7744	15.15

Source: DESHP.

In the foregoing paragraphs, the growth of infrastructural facilities, both absolute and relative to the growth of population/area of the State have been discussed. As noted earlier, the growth to these facilities, while contributing in some cases directly to the promotion of human welfare, is mainly seen as the index of the level of growth habits acquired by the economy.

CHAPTER 4

Anthropogenic Impact & Resource Utilization

The basic requirement fulfilment brought man to interact with environment. As the nature's course of yielding changed, man tried to modify its interaction for the fulfilment of its changing requirement. The real concern for interaction came about when the demand increased many-fold and natural bounty seemed to be falling short. The cultural tool empowered homosapiens to encroach upon environment and make larger use of it. The economy changed from gathering and collecting stage to complex economic system stage through primitive agricultural practices. The hilly environment, however, has witnessed these developments on a smaller scale due to the weak agrarian base (Ahmad '85). Once a balanced man-land ratio was attained the process of change was very slow. The process of economic diversification was slower even.

The hilly areas also experienced a unique survival of older modes of economies from gathering to transhumance, shifting cultivation and caravan trading. Under such conditions, the process of development operates as a low key and the hilly areas are only marginally integrated with the developed economies of the plains (Ahmad '85).

Resource utilisation and management depend upon varied admixture of technologies and sociogenesis. A typical mountain environment with its unique resource endowment gives rise to specific cultural milieu to make use of locally available resources to the extent endowment permits. The cultural development apart from acting within constraints accepts challenges and modify and present themselves in a variety of ways enabling population to rise against challenges of nature. The local nature constraints of the hill regions of Himachal Pradesh have led its inhabitants to develop various indigenous technologies to combat specifications of the nature. This process that cultural adoption is dynamic and changes with the change in natural system and with the utilisation pattern expresses through change in population pressure and change in its quality of living. The ethnic adaptability is usually safe till the resources have not been put to the limits of fragility by consumption through foreign intervention. In both cases the sustainability of resources comes under question. Therefore, an appraisal of resource utilisation and pressure on them gain special significance for explaining the levels of development through human activities and adaptation mechanism. It is important to examine these systems, as well as the changes in the responses of mountain habitants over time, in the light of development, which will provide a basis for evaluating the positive and negative effects of such changes on the sustainable development of this mountain environment, viz. basic economic activities of typical mountain agriculture system (Shrestha and Kanwal '92).

Uniqueness of mountain system

Various elements of mountain system have their unique pattern of association and their specific linkages make them unique whose identification as an unit is of great significance for evaluation of human impact.

Inaccessibility in the form of mountain region, the skewed distribution of settlement on the hills of mountain give rise to a situation where their remoteness acquires great significance for the evaluation of any planning strategy and developmental mechanism. The remoteness of population—a natural adaptation to scarce resource distribution acted in accordance with natural law till the pressure of population was not high which resulted in degradation of resources. The marginal resources were found heavily utilised spot on the natural system.

The inaccessibility factor has rendered the state with subsistence economy. Agriculture, the dominant economic scenery of the state, has barely shifted from subsistence level and if at all, it is towards high value low weight. This is because Himachal people have resorted to the use of local cultivation techniques and traditional management practices. They use little fertilizer and dependency on capital input is insignificant. Thus because of closed system, created by inaccessibility, there are strong associations among the three important components namely crops, livestock and forestry (Shrestha and Kanwal '92).

The poor ratio of man-resource ushers man to a situation where it goes on to exploit marginal resources adding to the fragility of the delicate man-environment relationship. The extension of grazing activities are some examples leading to extension of vulnerability of the environment. Nevertheless, certain measures are also undertaken by man to mitigate the consequences of inpact. The bunding and afforestation in steep zones are some measures. In the case of Himachal Pradesh most of the activities which are undertaken to mitigate fragility operate at macro economic level where even state level or national level planning gains significance. The policies like traditional plantation, social forestry and strategies like 'Van Lagao Rozi Kamao', plant and earn livelihood, have gained significance in the recent years.

Man tends to flock and concentrate on the situation where it can get maximum output by minimum effort and only turns towards less bountiful region when scarcity sets in. The scarcity is the reflection of less availability of resources per unit area or population and also the harbinger of marginal resource utilisation. The marginal resource of land emerges when forest is converted into various other uses in several parts of Himachal Pradesh. The small scale farmers have practiced high intensity of cultivation which also increases the fragility.

Along with fragility and marginality Himachal Pradesh presents itself with diversity in its ecological system. It acts to guide the resource users to result a particular use pattern. Sometimes it acts as forbidding factor, negating a particular use but at times presents with added endowment, e.g., cool climate for better use of it.

The natural constraints get reflected on economic development. An economic appraisal identifies two sets of constraints—one which is the constraint of institutional nature and the second includes the constraints that prohibit widening of production possibilities.

The amalgamation of thirty princely states into one unit was a major institutional constraint. They apart from having a few similar institutional units had a larger number of institutions quite unknown to other areas. This was a great impediment for the planners what they faced in the early years of growth. The institution of special groups of population like scheduled caste and scheduled tribes which account for about a quarter of its total population also required special treatment of status in view of economic situations. This has been the one area which the planners have not yet overcome.

The production possibility must be looked from the point of view where the basic requirements of people are fulfilled. The situation in this regard also does not seem bright as in an agrarian economy it is land which is basic of all production activities which is in short supply in Himachal Pradesh. About thirty per cent of the area is 10,000 feet and above. The state has relegated them to non-economic use also. The cold desert also accounts for a large area where six-month snow cover makes it unavailable for the cultivation and the rest of state does have other problems like low temperature, aspect, rocky character and undulation, etc. This makes available of only 15 per cent land of the total area of state for agriculture and other allied activities. Besides, the small pieces of land presents hurdle for the application of modern farm technology. Irrigation facilities have not been fabricated owing to topography. Apart from these resistances certain tacit bottlenecks are also operating like overhead maintenance of facilities is very high and low population density makes it even more costly. The short productive man year also presents great pressure on both the resources and the users.

Anthropogenic adaptability of specificities

The mountain environment specificities set only a broad framework within which anthropogenic activities operate choosing the opportunities at hand. This gives rise to diverse anthropogenic activities within identifiable varied framework. These framework in turn reflect both the positive and negative impact of anthropogenic activities according to which they alter and modify themselves. The development strategy working through anthropogenic activities on the mountain environment makes use of the resources to combat such constraints.

Population pressure

The basic anthropogenic impact assessment involves the assessment of human resource base. The assessment is made with regard to the positive as well as negative impacts which are rendered by the users on the used. The changes taking place on the need pattern merit to be evaluated on temporal scale for it has great bearing on all resources. Through various expressions human resource base exhibit their level of development in spatial context too. Thus emphasis has been on the evaluation of human resources at district level.

However, the growth rate of population has been rather slow in the case of Himachal Pradesh as compared to all India figure. The decennial growth rate of population of Himachal Pradesh has been affected mostly by external factors like influx of refugees and addition of new areas to it. Table 4.1 provides a picture of the population growth trend of Himachal Pradesh.

TABLE 4.1

Population growth in Himachal Pradesh

Year	Population (million)	Decennial variation (million)	Decennial growth rate (per cent)
1901	1.920		
1911	1.897	- 0.023	- 1.22
1921	1.928	+ 0.101	+ 1.65
1931	2.029	+ 0.101	+ 15.23
1941	2.263	+ 0.234	+ 11.54
1951	2.386	+ 0.123	+ 5.42
1961	2.812	+ 0.426	+ 17.87
1971	3.460	+ 0.648	+ 23.04
1981	4.280	+ 0.820	+ 23.71
1991	5.111	+ 0.831	+ . 19.39

In about four decades after the inception of Himachal Pradesh, the population has grown more than 125 per cent. The stability in population growth came about only in the seventies with the decline in external factors of population growth. Not only this but also the growth rate declined even during 1981-91. As far as spatial analysis is concerned, at district level the growth of population has been rather skewed which is evident from Table 4.2. In one district the growth has been negative much earlier during 1971-81.

The density of various genre explains the availability of resources to per unit of user as it is also an established method of assessing pressure. Land as a resource is very limited in Himachal Pradesh and for an agrarian economy it further has greater relevance. Both the densities, i.e. general (persons per

TABLE 4.2

Percentage growth rate of population

District	Percentage growth rate	
	1971-81	1981-91
Bilaspur	+ 25.58	17.7
Chamba	+ 23.23	25.6
Hamirpur	+ 18.85	13.0
Kangra	+ 20.56	16.0
Kinnaur	+ 18.70	19.1
Kullu	+ 24.30	26.3
Lahaul & Spiti	+ 16.31	(-) 3.9
Mandi	+ 24.46	19.1
Shimla	+ 20.95	20.3
Sirmaur	+ 24.85	23.4
Solan	+ 27.15	25.0
Una	+ 20.86	18.0

unit area) and agricultural (persons per unit cropped area) are considered for assessing the level of anthropogenic impact.

The density of population has a very high correlation with the distance from the plain. The closer districts have invariably recorded higher density of population and as one travels towards hill region the population density goes on declining. It can also be explained by the fact that availability of level land for cultivation goes on declining from south and south-west to north and north-east. Table 4.3 gives spatio-temporal picture of population density of Himachal Pradesh.

Undoubtedly, there is greater clustering of population in favourable areas without significant diversification of economy. Therefore, it has imposed burden on both the quality of environment in terms of agricultural land and forest resources and the quality of life (Kayastha '85).

The analysis of any change in rural population holds greater relevance in an agrarian economy like Himachal Pradesh. This is because any change in it will be reflected in the changes in

TABLE 4.3

Density and percentage of total population

District	1971		1981		1991	
	Den-sity	% of total popula-tion	Den-sity	% of total popu-lation	Den-sity	% of total popula-tion
Bilaspur	163	5.63	210	5.18	250	5.70
Chamba	31	7.38	48	7.31	60	7.65
Hamirpur	-	-	282	7.45	321	7.03
Kangra	155	38.35	168	23.17	200	22.50
Kinnaur	8	1.44	9	1.38	11	1.39
Kullu	35	5.56	43	5.57	55	5.90
Lahaul-Spiti	2	0.68	2	0.75	2	0.60
Mandi	128	14.89	162	15.09	195	15.40
Shimla	153	6.27	99	11.96	120	12.30
Sirmaur	86	7.08	108	7.20	134	7.41
Solan	-	-	156	7.11	196	7.42
Una	-	-	205	7.18	243	7.33

TABLE 4.4

Rural population as percentage of the total

District	1961	1971	1981	1991
Bilaspur	95.20	95.02	95.31	94.26
Chamba	92.16	92.59	93.13	92.39
Hamirpur	-	-	94.97	93.68
Kangra	96.05	96.28	94.75	95.11
Kinnaur	100.00	100.00	100.00	100.00
Kullu	96.80	94.40	92.95	92.97
Lahaul & Spiti	100.00	100.00	100.00	100.00
Mandi	94.40	89.65	92.64	92.70
Shimla	67.28	68.09	84.25	79.57
Sirmaur	92.78	91.52	91.23	89.95
Solan	-	-	89.19	87.53
Una	-	-	92.24	91.38

various sectors of economy. The change in rural population density of the state has not been significant over the last four censuses which is evident in Table 4.4.

Further study of it reveals the fact that the decline in per unit rural population was maximum in Shimla which naturally has added to the urban primacy of Shimla. A closer look brings forth the fact that Himachal Pradesh has an inverse relationship between altitude and density and positive relationship between rural density and remoteness from the plains. The obvious reason for decline in density with altitude is the cumulative effect of the environmental factors which determine the limit of human habitation. These factors include variability of climate and degree of slope with changing altitude, which renders land unfit for agriculture (Ahmad '90).

The real picture of crowding in economically significant areas is revealed by the high agricultural density which varied from 179 to 1270 persons per square kilometre in 1981, while it ranged from 155 to 691 persons in 1971. Surprisingly Lahaul & Spiti, with mostly barren tracts where agricultural land is highly restricted to a few small agricultural pockets in favourable valley areas, show the highest agricultural density of 1270 persons per square kilometre (1981). This makes living wretched on meagre agricultural resources and gives rise to numerous but peculiar socio-economic practices (Kayastha '85). The agricultural density has been rising constantly and as a result per capita availability of agricultural land is declining, which is evident in Table 4.5.

The spatio-temporal appraisal of agricultural density exhibits that it has continued to remain high in all the areas. The agriculture related anthropogenic activities when intense are likely to hammer the fragile environment. The remote areas, which have low density otherwise, also exhibit high agricultural density owing to limited agricultural land. This also adds to the misery of the environment. The absence of alternative opportunities of employment and means of earning livelihood,

TABLE 4.5

Agricultural density and area per capita of agricultural land (1981-91)

District	Physiological density ('81)	Cultivable area per capita ('81)	Physiological density ('91)	Agricultural area per capita ('91)
Bilaspur	716	0.139	891	0.112
Chamba	682	0.146	960	0.104
Hamirpur	179	0.558	930	0.107
Kangra	649	0.154	829	0.112
Kinnaur	623	0.160	921	0.108
Kullu	618	0.161	833	0.119
Lahaul & Spiti	1270	0.078	933	0.107
Mandi	677	0.147	798	0.125
Sirmaur	212	0.471	484	0.206
Solan	580	0.172	876	0.114
Una	635	0.157	830	0.122

has aggravated the pressure of high agricultural density. This calls for an urgent reorientation of the planning programmes giving emphasis on the development of secondary and tertiary sectors of the economy (Kayastha '85).

Harnessing the diversity of resource base

Among all the resource endowments of Himachal Pradesh, agriculture resource base is of prime importance. In all the four devised agroclimatic regions of Himachal Pradesh a variety of crops are grown. Regular crops are accompanied with a number of fruits and off-season vegetables. Ideal condition prevails for commercial livestock ranching. This diverse nature of its resource endowment singly contribute to the development of per capita income significant at state level when compared with other states.

TABLE 4.6

Landuse classification of area in each district (1988-89)

(In hectares)

District	Total geographical area by professional survey	Forest	Barren and unculti-vable land	Land put to non-agricultural uses	Culturable waste	Permanent pastures & other grazing lands	Land under tree crops and groves not included in area sown	Current fallows	Other fallow land	Net area sown
Bilaspur	116700	11253	6275	11862	4743	43045	104	1502	1105	32556
Chamba	651500	271568	4609	12010	5251	355993	358	2008	274	40348
Hamirpur	111800	19798	11854	17059	13343	359	—	8660	280	38561
Kangra	5739002	234467	52556	83563	47965	28858	1687	1517	—	126276
Kinnaur	655300	21479	84070	2806	1836	153559	96	1601	364	7582
Kullu	550300	—	4417	3990	2532	N.A.	323	2633	5	35842
Lahaul & Spiti	1369300	12832	4550	1634	543	192603	119	47	123	3176
Mandi	395100	160482	11462	11984	3757	111713	228	2597	204	95946
Shimla	513100	95430	14673	22371	10421	188157	3150	6918	1641	73728
Sirmaur	282600	48778	7632	9067	13257	62512	35281	4278	1011	42901
Solan	193700	19628	9971	10729	11839	80119	1626	3776	984	41649
Una	154000	28650	28548	19882	10921	6877	125	2979	11211	45006

On the way of resource utilisation fragility has its own expression level in terms of time and space. However, Himachal people have resorted to this problem by terracing, afforestation, orcharding and bunding, etc. to ameliorate the constraints to suit their needs.

The varied use of resources has brought to light other problems too. It creates a typical condition when nature eases the use of some resources while in some cases put impediments in the way of use of other resources. The external forces along with increased demand makes the situation more critical leading them towards alienation from the surrounding and give birth to fragile biodiversity.

Landuse

Land utilisation pattern explains the varied treatment of basic resources by mankind. Despite broader similarity in natural resource utilisation minor differences exist explaining the differential treatment. Their explanation gain special significance while explaining the anthropogenic impact in an agrarian economy, for it leads from the basic unit on which the economic activities take place and its significance goes high where it is less available. Table 4.6 gives an account of the landuse pattern in Himachal Pradesh.

The anthropogenic activities operate least in the initial stage of growth in economy in consequence with the natural factor. Himachal Pradesh, which has primarily an agrarian economy, includes most of its population whose activities vary with changes in agroclimatic system. The agroclimatic diversity holds promise to great variety in potential and production of various crops at different point of times in the year. The agroclimatic endowment, thus holds relevance for their comprehension to explain the anthropogenic activities in a better way.

Intra-Sectoral anthropogenic impact

Agriculture: Structural built-up

Prior to plan development era one may find little effort conceded on the part of government to better the agro-economic status of the people of Himachal Pradesh. The princely states and later the Britishers showed little interest in augmenting the economic structure which was very heavily dependent on land and cultivation which itself was on the mercy of natural factors. After four decades of Plan Development, the economy of Himachal Pradesh remained land-bound but with a promising base of agriculture, horticulture and forests with its allied activities.

Natural factors like climate, topography and soil, etc. have imposed great restriction on widespread practice of cultivation. Wherever these factors have been found favourable cultivation has been taken up in intensive way and as a result that has given rise to quasi-natural problem like soil erosion, fertility loss, drying-up of perennial streams.

Irrigation, one of the most important factors for intensive cultivation has posed a great constraint to intensification of cultivation. The level of irrigation not only explains the level of intensification of cultivation but also the level of anthropogenic interference as well as the level of economic development. The hypothesis is that more the intensity of irrigation better development of the region, for there has been a strong correlation between the intensity of cropping, resulting in high agricultural development consequent upon higher produced and the net area under irrigation. Areas under irrigation and source-wise allocation basically gives the idea of the extent of area where water has been used for irrigation but it in no way explains the intensity as large area may be due to larger area of that particular district. Intensity of irrigated cropping level thus also exhibits the level of advancement in agrarian eco-

TABLE 4.7

Intensity of irrigated cropping (1985-89)

District	1985-86	1986-87	1987-88	1988-89
Bilaspur	189.4	187.7	130.8	129.1
Chamba	192.0	192.8	179.6	159.8
Hamirpur	191.2	194.2	197.8	177.1
Kangra	198.0	200.8	211.9	198.9
Kinnaur	121.8	156.4	127.3	127.3
Kullu	100.0	100.0	100.0	100.4
Lahaul & Spiti	104.8	106.4	104.2	102.1
Mandi	186.1	191.2	178.4	179.5
Shimla	158.9	159.5	145.4	152.0
Sirmaur	180.0	186.0	158.9	158.6
Solan	157.8	153.4	158.9	158.6
Una	143.3	130.9	156.8	144.2
State	176.3	179.5	176.5	172.1

nomic structure. The intensity of irrigated cropping had mostly been more than 125 while for Kullu it is only a shade above 100. The change in middle order intensity has altered between 1985 and 1989 but for only lower and higher level intensities. Table 4.7 presents spatio-temporal changes in the intensity of irrigated cropping pattern in Himachal Pradesh.

Treatment of irrigation parameter in another form, i.e. percent of net area irrigated to net area sown explains a different picture altogether and it does not explain about economic advancement but brings into sharper focus the dependency on irrigation for agricultural activities. The two economically backward districts namely Lahaul & Spiti and Kinnaur record higher per cent of net irrigated area to net area sown exhibiting the lack of natural bounty. This fact emerges from the figures in Table 4.8.

In other words it also explains the reason why the aforesaid districts are lagging behind in agronomy. The respective change in major crops also exhibits how the variation have taken place in the field of irrigation during eighties.

TABLE 4.8

Percentage of net irrigated to net area sown in each district

Name of district	Percentage of net irrigated to net sown area 1970-71	76-77	80-81	85-86	88-89
Bilaspur	6.4	7.0	8.4	8.6	13.2
Chamba	11.7	11.2	11.3	8.4	8.8
Hamirpur	2.5	3.4	4.2	4.6	4.5
Kangra	30.1	31.4	27.3	26.3	25.7
Kinnaur	49.4	51.2	54.2	58.16	56.0
Kullu	6.4	7.7	7.3	6.2	6.3
Lahaul & Spiti	100.0	100.0	100.0	100.0	98.0
Mandi	14.7	16.4	16.3	14.9	14.6
Shimla	6.6	6.8	6.7	5.9	6.3
Sirmaur	21.5	24.7	25.8	31.1	32.4
Solan	16.0	17.2	18.0	23.0	23.6
Una	2.8	5.0	5.5	8.3	11.9

Another indicator which better explains the economic level as compared to irrigation which explained anthropogenic impact aptly, is the production of major crops at different spatial levels. Maize, wheat and rice are the major crops of Himachal Pradesh accounting for more than half of the total agricultural production. Maize is the most common food crop of the state grown with very low input of irrigation, fertilizer and other such factors. However, it has remained as principal crop for very long time and despite the relative growth of production of other crops it has not changed much. Himachal Pradesh ranks among five major states both in terms of yield and production of maize. Though it is grown all over the state, higher concentration is found in Kangra, Mandi, Solan and Sirmaur districts. Wheat accounts for half of the total foodgrain production of the state (1989-90). As far as area is concerned it is the most widely distributed crop in the state but higher production is concentrated in Kangra, Mandi, Shimla and Solan districts where higher input of HYV seed, fertilizer and irrigation has been made available. Still the productivity of wheat is lower than that of most other wheat producing states. Average yield per hectare was 1580 kg during 1989-90. Rice is the main crop of Kangra, Mandi, Shimla, Solan, Sirmaur and Bilaspur districts. Productivity of rice in Himachal Pradesh was 950 kg per hectare (1988-89). The cultivation of potato on commercial basis was introduced in mid 40s when import of seed potato stopped from Burma and other countries because of the second world war. With ideal climatic conditions for growing higher quality, disease-free seed potato, this crop proved highly successful. It immediately caught the fancy of the farmers and soon large areas came under this lucrative cash crop (M.G. Singh 1985). There has been no looking back since then and it is grown as seed crop in Shimla, Lahaul and Spiti districts where climate is ideal for quality production. Himachal is now also called as home of seed potato and its production which meets about 1/5th of the total seed requirement of the country is growing at a rate of more than 0.25 per cent per annum.

The great agroclimatic potentiality to grow vegetable for the market in plains has attracted farmers lately and in the areas where competition with the apple growing has been less, it has thrived well. This has been also boosted by the aid it has been receiving as it forms a part of the priority sector of the government. Agricultural scientists have also been constantly trying to develop varieties which best suit the climate of Himachal Pradesh. Like seed potato, seed vegetable has also been introduced and is getting popularity among farmers as it brings ready cash, for example the seed of cauliflower alone fetches farmers revenue of more than 1.65 crore rupees annually. Mushroom growing has a long history in Himachal Pradesh and it ranks high in terms of production of both seed and eatable types in the country.

Horticulture development

Various studies conducted in different agroclimatic regions of Himachal Pradesh prove that horticulture gives higher returns per unit of area as compared to basic agricultural crops. The economic planners also felt that instead of concentrating on cereal production more efforts should be made to accelerate the pace of development of horticulture, i.e. vegetables, vegetable seed production and allied items. As a result it was observed that horticultural development has proved helpful in supplementing the meagre income of the people of Himachal Pradesh. In the recent past, the production of temperate fruits, specially apple has gone a long way towards ameliorating the economic condition of the farmers. Keeping in view all these developments, a separate department of horticulture was established in 1970 so that concentrated efforts could be employed for its development and thereby bringing one-third of the cultivable land of the state under it.

Higher income generation from the production of temperate fruits like apples, peaches and plum made them lucrative. Sub-tropical fruits like many citrus fruits, mango, litchi and grapes are also gaining popularity in the state. The utilisation of areas unsuitable for ordinary crops like wheat, rice, maize, etc. are sometimes better suited for horticulture. About 1.5 lakh hectare land of Himachal Pradesh can be put to horticultural usages. Moreover, horticultural activities contribute soil conservation. It has been estimated that soil erosion in unprotected land can be restored as much as 50 tonnes per acre annually. Although exact statistics are not available, it may not be wrong to assume that thousands of acres of valuable land are being rendered useless annually on account of soil erosion in this mountainous land. Fruit trees check this problem. The erosion in orchards with soil under grass is almost negligible. Thus, the orchards make an important contribution towards increasing the production from areas which otherwise will be rendered unproductive. Fruit growing, therefore, helps tremendously the farmers in raising their income and also of the state by cutting the long term revenue wastage on soil conservation programmes. Apart from this there are a few indirect economic benefits that come alongwith its development like development of transport, marketing, processing industries and employment generation, etc.

Though the potentiality of growth of different fruits in Himachal Pradesh is immense throughout the state, certain areas are better suited for the growth of particular type of fruits. The major zonation of fruit types follow closely various altitudinal zone which is shown in Table 4.9.

TABLE 4.9

Zonation of fruit types

Approximate elevation range above sea level	Important fruits grown
1200 to 3000 feet (365 to 914 metres)	Subtropical fruits like litchi, loquat, guava, citru, citrus fruits, etc.
3000 to 5000 feet (914 to 1523 metres)	Stone fruits like peaches, plum, apricot, persimmon pear (hard and soft), pomegrannate, etc.
5000 to 9000 feet (1523 to 2742 metres)	Apple, cherry, pear (soft types), walnut, chestnut, etc.
5000 to 10,000 feet (1523 to 3656 metres)	Raisin, grape, prune, drying varieties of apricot, almond, chilgoza and apple, etc.

Apple which is by far the most important crop of the state was first commercially grown on modern lines in the second decade of the present century with the efforts made by an American (Mr. Satya N. Stokes). However, major progress was made after independence. Dry fruits are also grown in the districts of Kinnaur, Chamba and Lahaul & Spiti which have dry summer. They grow fruits like apricot, resin, grape, prune, almond, etc.

Various projects are underway for the scientific processing of horticultural products. A multi-crore project with the assistance of International Development Association (World Bank) is being implemented for setting up a large scale integrated system aimed at improving and processing of horticultural commodities. Under this project modern concepts of scientific marketing are being introduced, and a marketing infrastructure with 10 mechanised packing & grading houses, five cold stores in production areas, 20 kilometres of rope-way and one apple juice concentrate plant with a capacity to crush 18,000 tonnes of apples per year are being established. Under the World Bank Project a fruit processing factory with a capacity of 18,000 tonnes has been set up at Parwanoo.

Livestock resources

In a predominantly rural economy with vast fallow land development of livestock seems to be a logical consequence. Despite the Government's constant effort to reduce the herd size of non-improved stocks, their number has been constantly going high surviving on common property resources. The diversification of livestock in the recent year has increased which is evident from the fact that the per cent change of various group of livestock has been the maximum. The general growth in the livestock population in different districts of Himachal Pradesh can be said to be an indicator which would also reflect the live economic wealth of the districts which is shown in Table 4.10.

The government has been trying constantly the reduction of herd size, improvement of stock and adoption of stall feeding breeds. During 1991-92 cows numbering 2,05,000 and 30,000 buffaloes were artificially inseminated and the respective figure for such progeny born was 82,000 and 9600 respectively during the same period. During the same period there were 230 veterinary hospitals, 514 dispensaries and 89 outlying dispensaries functioning in the state.

To boost up stock improvement the demand of pure and cross breed bulls are met by five cattle breeding farms functioning at Kamand and Bhangrotu (Mandi), Kothipura (Bilaspur), Palampur (Kangra) and Bagthan (Sirmaur). The herd strength of animal accounts 339 only. However, in these farms, besides management, problem of exotic animals are studied there. There are three semen banks with deep frozen laboratory and six liquid nitrogen plants, which provide semen to various artificial insemination centres in the state (DESHP '89).

For improving the quality of sheep and wool, government sheep breeding farms are running at Jeori (Shimla), Sarol (Chamba), Nagwain (Mandi), Tal (Hamirpur), Karchham (Kinnaur) and Choori (Chamba) which are supplying improved sheep to the farmers of the state.

The flock strength in these farms was 2289. During 1991-92 about 860 improved sheep were distributed to the farmers. There are five sheep extension centres in operation in Kothikohar (Kangra), Swar (Mandi), Bagipul (Kullu), Dodra Kawar (Shimla) and Choori (Chamba). Under the special live-stock production programme for sheep development, sheep at subsidized rates are supplied and loans for this purpose are also provided to the small and marginal farmers and agricultural labourers in Sirmaur district. The production of wool was 15.67 lakh kg (1991-92). Angora Rabbit farms, for distribution of rabbits to the breeders, are functioning at Kandwari (Kangra) and Nagwain (Mandi). Poultry, another major live economic resource of the state has acquired significance in the recent past. There are 14 poultry farms functioning in the state which provide 42,000 eggs and 50,000 chicken for table and 2,10,000 bird and 5000 eggs for hatching (1991-92). The chicken and eggs production during the same year have been 2,64,200 and 3,40,700 respectively. However, the number of farms has been quite small considering the demand and efforts which are ongoing to establish 130 poultry units in the state during 1991-92.

Forest utilization structure

Climatic condition, low population density and ecological

TABLE 4.10

Livestock and poultry

Districts	Cattle		Change	Buffaloes		Change	Sheep		Change
	1977	1987	%	1977	1987	%	1977	1987	%
Bilaspur	60657	66370	9.41	67912	75132	10.63	33024	34154	3.42
Chamba	235810	247116	4.79	31449	34718	10.39	273880	269923	- 1.44
Hamirpur	68177	70447	3.32	72351	80328	24.65	49119	58877	19.86
Kangra	391482	419122	7.06	123657	138328	11.94	78618	90833	15.53
Kinnaur	21687	22352	3.06	"	5	- 54.54	51910	47168	- 9.13
Kullu	157961	153425	- 2.87	1615	1896	17.39	109877	111719	1.67
Lahaul & Spiti	9094	7652	- 15.85	—	—	—	42884	43233	9.71
Mandi	378752	393342	3.85	87103	89886	3.19	180954	194021	7.22
Shimla	333915	336653	0.81	19766	18589	5.95	151323	164958	9.01
Sirmaur	229150	224140	- 2.18	32622	34437	5.56	42468	38832	- 8.56
Solan	139614	150596	7.86	65886	64341	15.21	26194	25429	- 2.92
Una	79921	82448	3.16	67634	78755	16.44	9754	11175	14.56
Himachal Pradesh	2106220	2173663	3.20	560006	616415	10.07	1055005	1090322	3.34

Contd.

TABLE 4.10 CONTD.

Districts	Goats		Change	Others		Change	Total livestock		Change	Poultry
	1977	1987	%	1977	1987	%	1977	1987	%	1977
Bilaspur	59764	60893	1.88	530	1033	94.90	221887	237582	7.07	18275
Chamba	166316	173169	4.12	2068	2223	7.49	709523	727149	2.48	41660
Hamirpur	31783	39350	23.8	812	1234	51.97	222242	250236	12.59	17186
Kangra	131825	148425	12.59	9278	12726	37.16	734860	809434	10.14	93822
Kinnaur	18399	20148	9.50	3324	4196	26.23	95331	93869	- 1.53	3897
Kullu	56658	63032	11.24	1380	2242	62.46	327491	332314	1.47	10693
Lahaul & Spiti	12106	11422	- 5.65	4983	5716	14.71	74067	68023	- 8.16	1817
Mandi	200312	189796	- 5.24	3002	4048	34.84	850123	871093	2.46	39378
Shimla	98183	104011	5.93	4348	6484	49.12	607535	630695	3.81	54099
Sirmaur	104827	108482	3.48	3728	4385	17.62	412795	410276	- 0.61	20167
Solan	36672	74825	104.04	3547	2512	-29.17	311913	317703	1.85	15263
Una	68492	66309	- 3.18	1658	1579	-10.79	227459	240166	5.58	13304
Himachal Pradesh	1035337	10559862	2.36	38658	48278	24.88	4795226	4988540	4.03	329561

requirement have all added up to endow Himachal Pradesh with vast forest resources (924.4 thousand hectare—1989). The forests are mostly on government land which also earn about 25 per cent of its revenue and provide employment to more than five lakh people and grazing pastures to 20 lakh animals. Apart from their economic value these are also of great significance for ecological balance in the region and down in the plain. The forest types of the state, i.e. coniferous, broad-leaved etc. are found along different climatic built-ups. Deodar, Kail, Chil, Spruce, Silver fir and Neoza pine are the coniferous species growing in Himachal forest. Among the broad-leaved species, Sal, Bam oak, Morhu oak, Kharshu oak, Walnut, Maple, Bird cherry, Horse chestnut, Poplar, Seemal, Tun and Seesam are the important species growing in the forest. The regional distribution of forests at district level can be understood better from river basins area-wise. The river basin area and forest correspond closely with altitudinal zones, which are shown in Table 4.11.

TABLE 4.11

River basin area under forest at district level

District	Name of the river	% forest area in altitudinal zones					
		Below 1000	1000 to 1500	1500 to 2500	2500 to 3000	3000 to 4000	More than 4000
1	2	3	4	5	6	7	8
Bilaspur	Sutlej	91.4	8.6	-	-	-	-
Chamba	Ravi	4.3	6.7	33.2	18.7	23.1	13.9
	Beas	17.5	33.3	41.8	5.3	2.0	-
	Chenab	-	-	3.8	11.6	21.7	62.9
	Total	4.1	6.8	29.3	16.6	21.7	23.1
Hamirpur	Sutlej	97.5	2.5	-	-	-	-
	Beas	96.0	4.0	-	-	-	-
	Total	96.4	3.6	-	-	-	-
Kangra	Beas	58.9	5.8	8.5	4.1	9.2	12.6

Contd.

1	2	3	4	5	6	7	8
Kinnaur	Sutlej	-	1.2	16.3	15.3	26.3	50.8
Kullu	Beas	-	3.3	17.0	13.1	23.4	43.2
	Sutlej	2.2	14.4	42.0	23.7	13.9	3.8
	Total	0.4	5.3	21.5	15.0	21.7	36.2
Lahaul & Spiti	Chenab	-	-	-	2.3	21.5	76.2
	Sutlej	-	-	-	-	12.1	87.9
	Total	-	-	-	1.2	17.1	81.7
Mandi	Sutlej	19.6	30.2	46.6	3.4	0.2	-
	Beas	17.5	38.3	33.5	9.5	1.3	-
	Total	18.1	35.7	37.6	7.6	0.9	-
Shimla	Sutlej	7.7	25.2	39.5	15.9	8.5	3.3
	Yamuna	0.8	10.3	36.9	27.9	17.8	6.2
	Total	3.2	15.4	37.8	23.8	14.6	5.3
Sirmaur	Yamuna	28.0	53.7	12.1	3.1	-	-
Solan	Yamuna	4.7	54.2	41.0	-	-	-
	Sutlej	52.3	40.3	7.4	-	-	-
	Total	47.3	41.7	11.0	-	-	-
Una	Sutlej	99.3	0.7	-	-	-	-

The forests of Himachal Pradesh have been exploited to produce mainly timber. But due to the lack of infrastructure such usages have resulted in wastage of valuable wood which otherwise could have been utilised to feed wood-based industries to manufacture high value products. The forests of Himachal Pradesh have mainly been put to primitive usages resulting in great wastage of valuable wood which could otherwise be utilised to feed wood-based industries to manufacture newsprint pulp, plywood, etc., which are in short supply in the country. The exploitation which is very little mechanised results in great wastage of wood. Mechanisation only started as part of Third Five Year Plan in Rohru and Kullu Forest Division. With the introduction of these improved techniques, out turn of Spruce and Fir has almost doubled, while that of

Deodar and Kail has been increased by about 50 per cent. Besides modern exploitation, setting up of suitable wood-based industries is also essential to ensure better utilisation of available resources and increase employment opportunities for the population. Coniferous wood occurring in this state are exploited as raw material for the manufacture of number of products like newsprint, long fibre chemical pulp, rayon grade pulp, etc.

Out of the total production of about 35 per cent resin comes from Himachal Pradesh. Two Government resin and turpentine factories at Nahan and Bilaspur are capable of handling about 11,000 tonnes of resin.

Apart from resin, Himachal Pradesh has several other minor produce. Various medicinal plants are found in the state used for the manufacturing of alkaloid. The economic value of various minor produce has been growing (Table 4.12).

TABLE 4.12

Minor forest product

(Value in unit '000 Rs.)

Products	1982-83	1984-85	1986-87	1988-89
Bamboo & Canes	2197	1939	87	-
Drugs	360	353	4008	4955
Fodder & Grazing	1095	667	1955	622
Gram other than fodder	454	676	662	642
Gums & Resins	15902	20563	15432	15737
Others	92	66	167	32
Total	20100	24264	22311	21988

The pattern of utilisation of fuelwood exhibits close correspondence with agroclimatic zone. The per capita requirement in four agroclimatic zones is 0.8, 1.5, 2.5 and 4 tonnes/annum. The total requirement in the state is nearly 5 million tonnes. The energy plantation is only viable by identification of viable location which has been put forward.

The total land area under plantation comes to 32,16,900 hectares (Table 4.13). On the assumption that 50 per cent of this area is available for successful raising of such plantations and the annual biomass out turn, with a cycle of 10-12 years fixed at five tonnes/hectare/annum, the total fuelwood production shall be to the tune of 8.04 million tonnes/annum, which is fairly good to meet the demand to fuelwood.

TABLE 4.13

Area under plantation

Species-based forest	Plantation	
	Area planted during 1961-62 and 1984-85	Area planted upto 1988
Devdar	52262	63303
Kail	5921	7668
Fir/Spruce	9869	11315
Chir	145726	176568
Other Conifers	108	108
Walhed/nut	2056	2406
Willow	2847	3868
Mapple	93	93
Khair	78658	95409
Shiam	3405	4785
Bamboos	1368	1850
Mulberry	1272	1272
Poplar	2789	5895
Rubonia	7418	11982
Other broad leaved species	65960	93008
Total	379752	479620

Mining

The mineral resources are of great significance for the development of economic well being of any region. The tertiary development in a region must use the locally available resources to compete in the cost of production with other regions. Himachal Pradesh has proved resources of various minerals but only a few have so far been exploited due to poor infrastructural facilities available and the agrarian nature of the state economy. The mineral resources, which are exploited to a significant level are under consideration in the following paragraphs

Limestone: Limestone, one of the basic minerals used in different industries is found at Gagal and Barmana with a calcium oxide content of nearly 50 per cent. The reserve in areas are estimated to be 120 million and 30 million tonnes, respectively. Another belt of limestone is in Sirmaur district at three different places. Khari with a proven reserve of 12 million tonnes supports a cement plant at Rajban. The second and the third belts are Krol belt near Kamraso and Bharli areas of Namra limestone belt with very high grade calcium carbonate with more than 95 per cent. Chamba district has also recorded some medium grade limestone (about 50 per cent) Cao at Broh and Shind areas with estimated reserve of 350 million tonnes. Limestone is also mined in small quantities at Kangra, Solan and Mandi districts.

Gypsum: Sirmaur district has gypsum mines at Korga and Bhrall with reserve of more than 4 million tonnes in total. Another location of low grade gypsum is at Kuthar in Solan which is not being mined due to high cost of production. Another such mine is at Bathri in Chamba which is also not being exploited for the same reason. Remoteness and depth of occurrence are the major causes of non-exploitation of gypsum minerals from Kinnaur and Lahaul and Spiti.

Barytes: Barytes is found in the Kanti, Misswa, Tatyana, Dhala, Pipli and Tillardhar areas of Sirmaur district. An estimated reserve of 15,000 tonnes of barytes had been reported in Kanti-Tatyana areas. Availability of barytes in Naldera near Shimla has also been recently reported. The occurrence of barytes in Himachal Pradesh has been in the forms of veins and lenses. However, some of the less economically feasible resources are not under production.

Rock salt: Himachal Pradesh has distinct position in India as Mandi district is the only so far known source of rock salt in the country. However, rock salt is not exposed to the surface but its association with other exposed rock indicates its presence and places like Guma and Drang. Keeping in view the chemical properties of it, plans are ongoing to set up chemical industries near the mine.

Silica sand: Another resource in which the state abounds is friable quartzite boulders and pebbles which is found in some of the Khads and Nullahs of Una district. It is a good source of silica sand used for the manufacture of glass. Detailed investigations have proved the existence of more than one million tonnes of such boulders in Palkawa, Haroti, Homa in Una district. Bilaspur records presence of white quartzite which is used for the manufacture of the glass. The important localities in Bilaspur district where such deposits occur are Nihari, Chenala and along the valley of river Sutlej.

Oil and natural gas: Seepage of natural gas at Jwalamukhi, discovery of oil-impregnated sand stone at Chamukha near Sundernagar and availability of natural gas in the Tanlog tunnel and excavation near Rainka suggest the possibility of finding natural gas in these belts. The ONGC undertook two locations for deep drilling to a depth of 4,000 to 4,500 metres at Deoth Sidh in Hamirpur district and at Ramshar in Solan district where possibilities of oil reserve is fairly high.

Mineral water: Himachal Pradesh has been in news for mineral water availability. A small village near Palampur, called Sulah was discovered to have water of Medicinal properties and at present thousands of gallons are pumped out to cater the demand of people who flock there from all over the country. Another old spring at Kalath near Manali also records one of the best mineral waters in the world. The chemical analysis of the water reveals that it contains sodium, magnesium, calcium chloride, sulphates, phosphates and iron, besides carbondioxide as a gas. It registers a temperature of 39 degree centrigrade at the surface.

Other minerals: Various other minerals like megnesite (Bharmaur), radio active minerals (Parvati valley), pyrite (Chamba and Shimla), iron (Kangra, Kullu and Mandi), copper (Chamba and Kullu), mica (Kinnaur) and lead (Kullu and Solan) is found which make the state one of the rich states in terms of mineral deposits. However, remoteness, high cost of minerals, low infrastructure, small local consumption are some of the hurdles responsible for low contribution by them to the overall economy of the state. Nevertheless, their significance in contribution has been rising over time (Table 4.14).

TABLE 4.14

Value of minor minerals

(Value in '000 Rs.)

Minerals	Value		
	1985-86	1987-88	1988-89
Salt	636	2239	1795
Building Stones	1301	8446	24900
Limestone	19270	22939	132290
Bayrium	508	237	25970
Clay	—	157	180
Sand	1227	641	8400
Shale	—	5	1311
Slate (Nr.)	671	1028	115000
Boulder	93	261	20100
Barytes	—	70	70
Gypsum	—	143	100

Industry

As an ideal character of agrarian economy of the developing nations, Himachal Pradesh has recorded very small level of industrialisation. Whatever industry has developed, they are mainly of small scale nature, and mostly agro-based. Traditional crafts such as shawl making, wood work, etc. have taken the form of household industry after the independence with a general lack of large scale industries. The nature of topography, low economic level and lack of infrastructural development like transportation, etc. were a few earlier reasons which caused very slow development before Independence. The industrial growth recorded major thrust only after integration of the hill areas of Punjab with Himachal Pradesh in 1966. Some of the earlier industrial complex included the once set up at Solan and Paonta Sahib. The industries included light engineering goods and agro processing activities. The subsequent effort in the government plans included the establishment of small and cottage industry units based on locally available raw material to cater to the local requirements.

The industrial development started recording diversification on the basis of varied endowment of the region and requirements. Various governmental and semi-governmental organisations like the Himachal Pradesh Mineral and Industrial Development Corporation, the Himachal Pradesh Small Industries and Export Corporation, the Himachal Pradesh Agro Industries Development Corporation, the Himachal Pradesh State Forest Corporation, the Himachal Pradesh Fruit Processing and Marketing Corporation and the Himachal Pradesh Handicrafts and Handloom Corporation have contributed to the development of industries in Himachal. Central and state incentives are also available to the entrepreneurs setting industries in remote areas and priority sectors and as a consequence industries are coming up in the areas of fertilizer production, paper and pulp production, cement, chemical, food processing and light engineering goods production, etc.

The industrial development which takes place in accordance with the factors responsible for their growth often lead to the development of lop sidedness. Government at state level has been trying to develop various complexes so that a more balanced pattern of industrial development takes place, unlike natural growth. Such industrial estate with infrastructural facilities include the ones at Solan, Parwanoo, Barotiwala, Dharampur, Una, Mehatpur, Jawali, Dera Gopipur, Kangra, Paonta Sahib and Bilaspur. Others are also being set up at Nagrota, Bhagwan in Kangra district and Shamshi in the Kullu district. The incentives provided by the state government for setting up new industrial units include acquisition or provision of land at reasonable prices according to priority in respect of allocation of building material subsidy or interest for small scale industries, etc. Apart from the efforts of developing estate, the demarcation of whole state in three categories of land is another effort of government to mitigate industrial imbalance. The A Class industrial areas include Paonta Sahib, Parwanoo, Solan, Nallagarh, Mehatpur, Kundori and Sansarpur, etc. The C grade areas comprise the tribal belts. The areas not included in A and C categories are considered as B grade areas. Apart from these area types, industries have also been classified on other basis in Himachal Pradesh. Government gives priorities to industries which are employment generating

TABLE 4.15

Number of SSI units registered on permanent basis

District	1984-85	85-86	86-87	87-88	88-89	89-90
Bilaspur	111	119	104	113	130	100
Chamba	75	87	98	81	110	65
Hamirpur	83	91	93	116	90	100
Kangra	302	276	292	286	241	247
Kinnaur	46	45	44	34	38	26
Kullu	80	74	90	97	137	84
Lahaul-Spiti	34	40	33	18	17	16
Mandi	146	151	154	100	111	122
Sirmaur	78	159	133	134	133	115
Solan	158	124	5	130	220	124
Una	193	202	—	91	94	123

and in which value addition is high. The policy is not positive but also restrictive for it checks industries in the areas which are environmentally not keeping well. Various government incentives were being given in terms of 15 per cent subsidy but after declaring Himachal Pradesh as 'No Industrial State' it went up to 25 per cent and in certain cases up of 33 per cent. But despite the efforts of government, natural factors of growth have contributed more to the development of industries in a less uniform fashion. However, the growth in different districts has been less similar in terms of change in small scale industrial units (Table 4.15).

Tourism

The scenic beauty and favourable climatic set up favours Himachal Pradesh to emerge as a region greatly sought after among tourists—national and international. The resultant tourist sector has been rightly adopted by the planners as an industry. As a result this industry has developed manyfold in the recent past.

Himachal Pradesh Tourism Corporation has been constantly trying to develop this sector through its various programmes. Among the priority sectors are the foreign tourist, adventure sports, development of roads near existing highways and development of facilities in the interest of the region. Himachal Pradesh has more than 35 tourist centres connected with all weather roads.

CHAPTER 5

Appraisal of Government Planning and Strategies

The undulating terrain of the Himalayas have always been considered impregnable which is why its population has been isolated and away from the mainstream. It was during the British time that planned resorts came up in the hills. These places offered many advantages to them like ensuring privacy, supply of cheap domestic labour and refuge from oppressive heat of the plains. The gradual increase in the population in this mountainous area posed many problems for largely the tribal people of the area. The problems compounded when a similar methodology for evolving planning strategies were adopted for plains as well as for the mountainous area. This sort of uniformity in dealing with two different areas with different situations has also led to the mutation of planning genetics of Himachal Pradesh. There is a need to deal with the problem of hills separately in strict sense so that the advantages of the specialisation and technology of the present age can be judiciously utilised.

The main constraints before development activities in the hill areas are the complexity of its physical features and climate which lead to a certain type of economy, obstructive communication and vulnerable ecology. Majority of the population is engaged in subsistence agriculture with little signs of modernization. However, a sizeable population has taken up horticulture which is favoured by the condition of the area.

The emphasis is also laid on the development and management of forest, pasture and orchard as a result Himachal has become a leading state in apple growing which is financed largely by the World Bank. However, it is also essential to assess the area and productivity potential of the fruits so as to evolve a suitable strategy for their proper development.

The establishment of industries is another significant factor which poses different set of problems in this mountain land because of the terrain, danger of pollution, inaccessibility due to the lack of transport along with low population density.

Roads are the life line of economy without which there will not be a proper orientation of development. Therefore long term plan need to be followed to put development on road.

Himachal Pradesh has a vast hydrological network with five major river systems. Besides this, there are springs and lakes adding to the water wealth but it is the major snow fed rivers and their tributaries which are being utilised for hydel generation. The hill areas pose different problems in terms of irrigation as compared to plain areas. Besides the gravity flow in most of the irrigation schemes is provided only with the help of high lift system for which availability of cheap hydroelectric power is essential. The harnessing of its potential water resource will not only provide irrigation but also cheap hydroelectricity which will discourage deforestation by fulfilment of fuel needs of the masses.

Government as an agency is the most important institution which guides most profound anthropogenic impact on the ecosystem. The welfare character, consistent need for economic development, infrastructure extension and overall commitment makes government and its allied agencies unparallel in terms of their denting capabilities. Government makes impact through the tools of its various policies and strategies which give rise to differential pattern of anthropogenic impact and economic development. The major issues which are responsible for the differential generation are put to question. The major sectors where impact reflects fast and vividly and where intensity of institutional effort is high, include forestation, power generation, land reform and wasteland development, livestock development and various such projects, which are put to study here.

Afforestation

Forests have played a very significant role in the economy of Himachal Pradesh as they grow primarily on their own where most of the economic expressions find hard to survive. The forests have been taken as a very significant sector of development and their mere protection has not been taken as of paramount significance, but their judicious exploitation is also stressed. Various anthropogenic activities, reflected as anthronomic expressions in respect of forest of government is put to question for the status evaluation within the state.

Himachal Pradesh, the life source of general major rivers of the country requires a thick vegetal cover in its catchment area. This feature makes the state to gain importance in respect of forest not only for the local people but millions of people dependent on the rivers in the plain. Realising its responsibilities the state government in collaboration with various other bodies has taken afforestation programme at a large scale (Table 5.1).

TABLE 5.1

Plantation in Himachal Pradesh

Period	Area planted (in hectares)
1961-69 (Including annual plans between 1966 and 1969)	83,822
1970-75	81,865
1975-80	1,09,763
1980-85	1,28,921

The state and central assistance have also been rising for afforestation and only in between Sixth and Eighth Plans the value of planted trees rose from Rs. 3759.9 lakhs to Rs. 24,000 lakhs, which explains the importance, the government accords to this.

Afforestation in the state is undertaken largely through productive forestry scheme and National Social Forestry, i.e. Umbrella Project. The former concentrates on fast growing species of high economic value and the major off shoot of the latter programme is called 'Van Lagao Rozi Kamao' Project. Nearly 2.5 thousand hectares of land was covered under productive forestry scheme with a cost of 168.72 lakh up to December 1991 and an area of 788 hectares have been covered during the same period under Social Forestry Scheme. Under 'Van Lagao Rozi Kamao' Scheme an additional 21.72 lakh plants were distributed up to December 1991. Under this programme Antodaya and other IRDP identified poor families are selected for plantation on government land and for looking after them. During first three quarters of 1991-92 an area of 8649 hectares was covered against the target of 15,028 hectares under this scheme. Under this programme 7000 families were associated for raising plantation and 2000 families had to raise nurseries of plants on their private land. Another major character of this programme was that the amount payable to forest planters was on the basis of survival percentage of the plants.

The forests have close relationship with their users—man and hence the change in the latter reflect, in most of the cases, a change in the former specially in an agrarian rural economy. The spatial variation of the density of population and the forest cover are important to explain the status of forest revenue in relation to population pressure which is evident in Table 5.2.

TABLE 5.2

Forest cover and population density

District	Density of population (81)	Forest cover 1000 hect. (81)	Density of population (91)	Forest cover 1000 hect. (90)	% Decadal change	
					Population	Forest
Bilaspur	212	10.5	250	11.2	17.9	6.6
Chamba	48	247.0	60	271.6	25.0	9.9
Hamirpur	284	18.2	321	19.8	13.0	8.7
Kangra	173	223.2	200	234.5	15.6	5.0
Kinnaur	9	12.6	11	21.5	22.2	70.6
Kullu	43	—	55	—	27.9	—
Lahaul & Spiti	2	12.6	2	12.8	0	14.2
Mandi	163	140.9	195	160.5	19.6	13.9
Shimla	100	56.5	20	95.4	20.0	68.8
Sirmaur	109	44.5	134	48.8	22.9	9.6
Solan	157	17.9	196	19.6	24.8	9.4
Una	206	26.2	243	28.7	17.9	9.5

Wasteland development

The land is a scarce resource in any hill region which can be put to economic uses hence the constant growth in demand has brought the marginal land under economic exploitation ignoring the ecological perspective. This led to the degradation of ecologically sound land into wasteland whose environmental degradation is reflected in various ways as impediment to further economic development. The area above 13,500 feet altitude is left uneconomic to be used. The situation in various parts of the state has touched alarming level and natural ecosystem must be restored at a priority level. Table 5.3 gives an account of the altitudinal distribution of land which need to be given due consideration while aspiring any wasteland development programme.

TABLE 5.3

Altitudinal distribution of land

Altitudinal range	Area (sq. kms.)	% land area
Below 3000 feet (915 metres)	8,306	15
3000 to below 5000 feet (916 to 1525 metres)	8,433	15
5000 to below 8000 feet (1526 to 2440 metres)	7,633	14
8000 to below 10,500 feet (2441 to 3200 metres)	5,738	10
10,500 to below 13,500 feet (3201 to 4115 metres)	8,438	15
Above 13,500 feet (4116 metres and above)	17,125	31
Total	55,673	100

Erosion of soil needs to be checked for the development of wasteland. The increase in human population has pushed ahead the livestock population and, in turn, togetherly they have extended the marginal agricultural land for fuel, fodder and other uses. The landuse also got diversified with the introduction of activities such as horticulture, infrastructural diversification like roads, buildings, and dam construction leading to rise in pressure on the scarce land resource. The infrastructural development also had a snow-bowling effect on the landuse as the extraction of remote resources became viable. The government at various levels has been aiming at identification of wasteland and their potential for amelioration and exploitation of watershed on viable basis for wasteland development. Apart from that the basic requirement for which the land is degraded must also be fulfilled. This has guided majority of the planners to encourage fuelwood plantation, and horticulture development, etc. The average requirement of fuelwood in Himachal Pradesh is nearly six lakh tonnes per annum but accounted supply is barely over two lakh tonnes. Hence this requirement must be fulfilled by proper planning if incompatible environmental exploitation of forest and ultimately land degradation are to be checked.

Industries

Himachal Pradesh for its various constraints stemming from its history, has been a late starter in the field of industry. Post-independence and post-reorganisation phases have recorded some development in this sector and beginning was made through traditional crafts of high value. The present investment in the sector is nearly 300 crores and engages about 80,000 persons. Low bulk but with high value products have made inroad in this sector and their mushrooming in response to various incentive holds great promise for the future.

Keeping in view the spatial imbalances and geographical endowment the planners have identified various individual areas where basic facilities for setting up of industries are present. The industrial areas identified are Parwanoo, Barotiwala, Baddi, Paonta Sahib, Mehatpur, Shamshi, Nagrota, Bagwan, Bilaspur, Reckong, Peo, Sansarpur, Terrace, electronics complex at Solan (Chambaghat), Mandi, Kala Amb, Hamirpur, Shoghi, Chamba and Amb and the industrial estates at Solan, Dharampur, Kangra, Jawali, Dehra-Gopipur were established. This picture is still not of a balanced industrial state and the efforts are on to bring in newer areas in the industrial map of Himachal with suitable basic facilities for secondary and tertiary sectors' development (Table 5.4).

Himachal Pradesh is in its early stage of industrial development where government incentives are maximum and very cordial labour management relationship exists, hence fast growth is expected. However, remoteness of the areas are great

TABLE 5.4

Districtwise number of registered factories and workers

District	Factories						Workers					
	1984	1985	1986	1987	1988	1989	1984	1985	1986	1987	1988	1989
Bilaspur	77	84	85	85	85	86	560	569	619	619	619	639
Chamba	57	58	58	59	59	59	621	622	622	638	638	638
Hamirpur	129	152	153	159	161	161	225	225	305	337	343	343
Kangra	113	130	135	146	151	151	6540	6665	6865	7021	7091	7091
Kinnaur	7	8	8	9	9	9	164	264	264	309	309	309
Kullu	151	155	155	155	157	157	463	467	467	467	471	471
Lahaul & Spiti	—	—	—	—	—	—	—	—	—	—	—	—
Mandi	150	154	166	171	171	171	3577	3581	3806	3842	3842	3842
Shimla	117	121	122	125	127	127	1912	2124	2126	2135	2139	2139
Sirmaur	31	39	51	54	57	58	608	1058	4021	4136	4365	4465
Solan	162	197	220	230	235	240	5973	8538	10360	11185	11431	11511
Una	52	53	56	58	58	59	1780	1830	2117	2174	2174	2183

impediment which has to be overcome by fast development of transportation facilities. The small local market, rural base of economy, are the other minor obstacles on the way of industrialisation which can be easily overcome in due course of time. The region has also potentiality to develop sophisticated high skill products like engineering goods.

Power generation

Energy generation and consumption as indicators speak a great deal about the economic condition of the region. Himachal Pradesh due to the steep slope of the rivers has a vast scope for generation of hydel power which is going untapped in majority of the cases. The potentiality of which not only will meet the local demand but can also contribute to the eradication of power shortage throughout northern India. Himachal Pradesh in collaboration with various other states is vigorously trying to execute several large and small scale projects within its boundary.

The privilege the state has of the flowing of five perennial rivers which are unparallel in potential. The Chenab, Ravi, Beas, Sutlej and Yamuna, of which Sutlej is the largest river flowing through five districts, have all high hydro electricity generation potential in their upper courses. The snow-fed character makes them perennial; and the natural reservoirs and large drops available along the course of these rivers provide vast potentiality, i.e. nearly 8.5 million kilo-watt which is about 20 per cent of the total estimated power potential of the country. Out of the total potential 3369 mega-watt has been harnessed (272 mega-watt by state and rest by central agencies). There are different agencies bent upon exploitation of power resource, wherever they are eco-environmentally and feasible the details of which are given in Table 5.5.

TABLE 5.5

Major on-going hydel projects in Himachal Pradesh (1992)

Name of the project	Estimated cost (Rs. crore)	Location	Installed capacity
1. Thirot Hydel	34.00	Lahaul-Spiti	4.5 MW
2. Baner Hydel	35.65		12 MW
3. Gaj Hydel	35.82		10.5 MW
4. Bhaba Augmentation Scheme	16.33		54 KV
5. Kittar Hydel	1.73		300 KW
6. Uhl State III Project	173.96		70 MW
7. Larji Hydel	355.00	Mandi	126 MW
8. Nathpa Jakhri	1678.00	Ravi	1500 MW
			800 MW

Development of non-conventional energy

Himachal Pradesh despite the fact that it is best endowed with hydro-electric resources its other non-conventional sources cannot be underestimated. Several inherent problems in hydro-electricity like distribution and high installation cost makes the case of the non-conventional even more strong. The task of adoption, popularisation and awareness towards the development of non-conventional energy sources under 'Him Urja' which has distributed, by 1991, 15,775 smokeless chulhas, 11,182 portable chulhas, and 31,994 pressure cookers and 6,389 nutan stoves in the state. Rural electrification is an important sector of the government planning as majority of the population lives in rural areas. It is realised by the planners, that unless and until energy sources are not provided to the houses in the villages the cutting down of the forest cannot be checked. So, realising the importance of power sector, great effort was made and as a result a state like Himachal which was one of the tailenders in respect of rural electrification about four decades ago now boasts of being one of the forerunners. This progress is recorded in Table 5.6.

TABLE 5.6

Number of electrified villages

District	Total No. of inhabited villages	Number of electrified villages as on 31 March				% of village electrified up to 3/87	% of village electrified up to 3/88
		1985	1986	1987	1988		
Bilaspur	911	857	874	911	911	100.00	100.00
Chamba	1095	902	934	982	1984	86.68	100.00
Hamirpur	1619	1526	1607	1619	1619	100.00	100.00
Kangra	3974	3681	3810	3850	3858	96.88	100.00
Kinnaur	77	72	75	75	77	97.40	100.00
Kullu	169	132	136	161	169	95.26	100.00
Lahaul & Spiti	235	153	161	176	234	74.90	100.00
Mandi	2789	2116	2313	2569	2786	92.11	100.00
Shimla	2188	2044	2091	2156	2185	98.53	100.00
Sirmaur	965	867	904	947	965	98.13	100.00
Solan	2337	1789	1896	2143	2336	91.70	100.00
Una	557	475	515	552	554	99.10	100.00

Rural development

In a state where majority of population lives in rural areas, intensified efforts on the part of government is inevitable through various plans to constantly improve their lot. Growth in production, better distribution of income and reduction of unemployment are some of the major areas where intensified thrust of planning is being made. There are several plans for development and extended for the rural hill people of Himachal from Central and State assistance which go a long way in shaping economic level and monitoring anthropogenic impact.

Various sectors of economy work in close relationship with other sectors and development of a few of them often do more harm than benefit. Keeping these views in mind CDP was extended whose aim was integrated development. Education, cultural activities, basic infrastructure provision, diffusion of innovation of primary schools and basic health provision are some of the areas where integrated development is done at Panchayat level by providing grant-in-aid. Keeping in view the vast applicability area of the plans an amount of Rs. 127 lakhs was sanctioned under this scheme during 1991-92.

Rural sanitation

Rural sanitation is another thrust area whose significance was felt recently and a massive programme was launched in the state. The environmental and health aspect are greatly affected by sanitation and with this view latrines were constructed in rural households and in the community centres in the rural areas. The assistance provided to the beneficiary has been enhanced to Rs. 1200 for general category and Rs. 1500 for scheduled castes/tribes and antodaya families. Against a target of construction of 10,000 sanitary latrines by 1991-92 only a small share was achieved (i.e. 1100) by the end of year 1991. Awareness towards it is increasing and there is all hope that Rs. 9.59 lakh incurred under this scheme will contribute towards environment improvement.

Rural housing

Rural housing is also known as Two Room Tenement Scheme under which 192 houses were constructed upto December 1991. The Revenue Department identifies the target facilities. The achievement is not very impressive and it was only about 60 per cent by spending Rs. 14 lakhs against a sanction of Rs. 20 lakhs.

Government schemes

Integrated rural development programme (IRDP)

The majority of rural inhabitants of the state are farmers whose status improvement has been a prime concern of the central agencies. The centrally approved programme take in its ambit the improvement of small and marginal farmers, agricultural labourers and rural artisans below poverty line. Making the provision for the productive assets, subsidies and institutional credits are some of the *modus operandi* of this scheme. Nearly 10,000 families of the state were brought under this scheme to improve their lot with an assistance of over Rs. 285.25 lakhs. There are various plans extended as a part of IRDP like TRYSEM and DWCRA. TRYSEM or Training of Rural Youth for Self Employment is extended with the aim to provide necessary technical skill to rural youths of target group in the age group of 18-35 years to enable them to take up self employment ventures in the broad fields of agriculture and allied activities, industry, services and business activities. Training to the interested rural youths is imparted free of cost in various government training institutions like ITI's, Government Polytechnics and other local institutions. During training, the trainees are given stipend from Rs. 150 to Rs. 350 per trainee per month subject to the place of training. Besides, after the completion of the training a free tool kit is given to them. Up to December 1991, 1053 youths were trained, 504 youths were settled, 213 youths were provided wage employment and an amount of Rs. 20.29 lakhs has been incurred during the same period.

Development of women & children in rural areas (DWCRA)

DWCRA is aimed to increase employment opportunities for the rural women. It takes up new income generating activities on group basis acceptable to them. This scheme is operational in many parts of the state like in Kangra, Shimla,

Chamba, Mandi, Sirmaur, Kullu and Solan districts. By December 1991, out of 300 target groups 279 groups were made operational having the membership of 4639 women. Total outlay of Rs. 23 lakhs was needed in it.

Jawahar rozgar yojna

By merging the erstwhile programmes of NREP and RLEGP this Yojna came to light. It was launched throughout the country aiming at generation of larger employment opportunities for unemployed and underemployed youths in rural areas. Specially, it aimed at creating productive community assets for direct and continuing benefits to the poor sections of the society. This programme works at village panchayat level. By December 1991, it generated 19.20 lakh man days of employment against the target of 37.23 lakh man days of employment. It created 1837 community assets by the end of same period with an overall exchequer of Rs. 654.57 lakhs.

Indira awas yojna

This housing scheme partially funded by Jawahar Rozgar Yojna is also target group-oriented. The beneficiaries include the Scheduled Castes and Scheduled Tribes people who are below poverty line. Minor assistance drains into from the Rural Sanitation and Smokeless Chulha Schemes, too. The beneficiaries are provided with an assistance of Rs. 14,500 for the construction of houses. These houses are planned to have the facilities of sanitary latrines and smokeless chulhas. During 1991-92 period 200 houses were constructed against the target of 351 houses in which 38.71 lakh rupees were incurred.

Smokeless chulha programme

This centrally sponsored scheme aims at reduction of deforestation by saving fuel and improvement in the health of rural women by reducing the pollution. For this smokeless chulhas are installed in the households and awareness and training camps for rural masses are organised at different levels. By December 1991, a total number of 9911 chulhas were installed against the target number of 20,000 incurring Rs. 8.23 lakhs.

Desert development programme

Certain pockets of Himachal Pradesh like Spiti sub-division of Lahaul & Spiti district and Pooh sub-division of Kinnaur district, where cold desert prevails, special care is needed for their improvement. This centrally sponsored programme aims at integrated development with special thrust on the growth of productivity, high income level and employment opportunities. Under this programme preventive measures are also taken to check on further deterioration of desert environment. During 1991-92 a provision of 200 lakh rupees was made available for bringing 807.26 hectares against which only 614.50 lakh hectares could be covered.

Drinking water

The problem of potable water has escalated with the increase in demand. In Himachal Pradesh 11,887 villages have been declared as problem villages and 4920 as easy villages. By 31st March, 1985 drinking water facilities were provided to 1,02,634 villages comprising 8348 problem and 4286 easy category villages. During Seventh Five Year Plan 2621 villages were covered (2432 problem and 189 easy villages.). During 1990-91, 350 villages were covered which was expected to rise to 354 by 1991-92 with a provision of Rs. 30.55 crores. The central assistance to state government for the execution of this programme comes under Rajiv Gandhi National Drinking Water Mission. The old drinking water schemes in the state towns are quite old and inadequate to cater to the present needs. Keeping in view this urgency augmentation of water supply schemes for towns, 800 lakh rupees has been incurred. During 1991-92 a provision of Rs. 60 lakhs was provided for sewage and sanitation schemes.

Indo-German eco-development project (Changer area project)

As the name suggests, this project is run by international funding unlike the aforesaid programmes. Though their impact is limited they are not less profound. One such project is Dhauladhar Farm Forestry at Changer area of Palampur by the assistance of Germany with an estimated expenditure of Rs. 18.71 crores. The project caters major economic activities of the rural areas, viz. forestry, agriculture, horticulture and animal husbandry and integrates them for the balanced economic development. Rupees one million was provided for this purpose during 1991-92. The major activities so far undertaken include plantation, soil and water conservation, awareness on timber and fuel saving devices and adoption of improved techniques in agriculture, horticulture and animal husbandry practices.

World Bank aided watershed development project for Himalayan hills (Kandi project)

During 1990-91, this integrated watershed development project was launched at Kandi hills, with the World Bank assistance. This project aims at rehabilitation of the fragile catchment areas of five major rivers, to improve the socio-economic conditions of farmers living in these areas. Kandi area, where soils are highly eroded and are subjected to drought conditions throughout the year has also been included in this project area.

The project runs on multi-disciplinary approach hence integrates the developments of forest, agriculture, horticulture and animal husbandry. During 1991-92, 226 lakh rupees was incurred on plantation in an area over 3294 hectares, besides carrying out other soil conservation works and treatment of lands.

Thrust sectors: Agriculture

The leading role of agriculture in the economy of Himachal Pradesh needs special consideration while chalking out any plan and programme. It is the largest single industry providing employment to nearly three-fourth of the working population. The significance of this sector does not diminish if one considers it in the light of gross domestic product of which more than half of the total comes from this sector. Despite positive picture, this sector is not free from problems that hampers its growth. The population pressure increase has brought in some of the marginal areas under cultivation, which are not suitable for this purpose. This leads to severe degradation in most of the cases. The basic objective of agricultural planning which has occupied the minds of strategy makers is the self-sustained growth. An ideal plan need to be developed which can cope up with the various resistance like remoteness, low productivity, lack of available cultivable land has been brought under the plough and there is practically no scope for further extension of land for cultivation. Considering the agroclimatic condition of the state there are certain benefits in growing particular commercial crop and efforts are on to make them popular.

The agroclimatic condition of the state is best suited for growing the vegetable at a time when they are not grown in the plains; hence off-season vegetables like tomato, peas and cauliflowers can fetch handsome cash to the farmers in catering the demands of plains. Some of the vegetables, much in demand in plains during off-season have great potentiality and efforts are on in the state to increase their production during such season. 3.65 lakh tonnes of vegetables were grown in Himachal Pradesh during 1990-91 and the corresponding figure for 1991-92 was 3.68 lakh tonnes. Gigner and quality potato are two major vegetables in which the state ranks among toppers. Himachal Pradesh is the second largest ginger producing state of the country. It was 2.9 thousand tonnes during 1991-92. The chief producing districts include Sirmaur, Solan, Bilaspur, Kangra and Shimla. Due to suitable agroclimatic conditions good quality of seed potato is produced in Lahaul and Spiti, and Shimla districts, which is much in demand throughout the country. The production has been 1.25 lakh tonnes in 1991-92. Multiple cropping is another strategy which help in better exploitation of agronomic potential of the state.

The strategy aims at taking more crops per annum from the same land. Emphasis is laid to increase the intensity of cropping through better crop rotation, inter-cropping, relay-cropping, mixed-cropping, etc. With the introduction of high yielding varieties it has now become possible to adjust the duration of crops to fetch additional intermediate crops. The little possibility of extension of cultivable land gives extra attention to this crop season adjustment strategy. The multiple cropping has another advantage that farm labour is fully utilised besides full utilisation of the land. Thus, it helps the state by accelerating agricultural productivity and by providing employment to the people. The following are some of the crop rotations which are being adopted by the cultivators:

(i) Maize-Toria-Wheat-Moong
(ii) Maize-Toria-Potato
(iii) Maize-Potato-Potato, and
(iv) Maize-Potato-Wheat.

Another major sub-sector of agriculture is irrigation where immediate attention is being given. The major share of cultivated land (8.1 per cent) depends on the mercy of the weather and hence better adaptation of dry land farming on a priority basis was a logical consequence. By the year 1991-92 more than four lakh hectare of land was brought under such practices. Apart from that during the same period five watershed areas were identified for better management of the water resources to carry on irrigation in an area of 500 hectares. As far as funding is concerned, Rs. 270 lakhs was spent during 1990-91 to irrigate additional 250 hectares and during 1991-92, it incurred Rs. 1191 lakhs to bring another 300 hectares of additional land under irrigation. This shows that more difficult areas cost higher. There are a few other funding bodies also providing funds like USAID. There are certain other programmes like National Garden Development under USAID Hill Area programme.

Marginal farmers are aided financially to grow fruit plants (maximum of ten plants per family). Dry and other temperate fruits are being developed with assistance from Indo-Italian fruit Development Project in the areas of Kullu and Chamba. The Indo-Dutch Mushroom Development Project at Palampur is another such collaboration. In 1991, the production rose to 239 tonnes. Under the project in same year 20 farmers were trained. And thus, intensification of cultivation with more lucrative crop adoption is the guiding principle of the planners in the present age in Himachal Pradesh.

Chapter 6

Anthronomic Profile of Himachal Pradesh

The State Domestic Product (S.D.P.) is supposed to be one of the most important indicators for measuring the economic growth. The total State Domestic Product at 1980-81 prices increased to Rs. 1110.72 crores in 1990-91 from Rs. 1074.61 crores in 1989-90, thereby registering a growth of 3.4 per cent. The growth rate of Gross Domestic Product at national level during same period was 5.6 per cent. The reason for such a low growth rate of the state was mainly due to the significant decline in the production of apple and other fruits. The foodgrains production though increased to 14.3 lakh tonnes in 1990-91 from 13.7 lakh tonnes in 1989-90, apple production declined to 3.42 lakh tonnes in 1990-91 from 3.95 lakh tonnes in 1989-90 (DESHP '92). Due to strong dependence of economy on agriculture (30 per cent) the state income in 1990-91 resulted in a situation where the change in latter got reflected in the change in the former.

Table 6.1 shows the growth of economy of Himachal Pradesh *vis-a-vis* at all India level from 1986 to 1991. (See Table 6.1 on the next page).

The growth of the per capita income of the state which was fairly fast during mid-seventies saw decline during 1990-91. This again is explained by the less diverse nature of economy of the state. The extension and intensification of agriculture has nearly touched the climax wherein no more physical area may be added to the existing aereage. Hence any decline in productivity brings down the economic growth rate.

TABLE 6.1

Annual economic growth rate

(In percentage)

Year	Himachal Pradesh	All India
1986-87	7.3	3.6
1987-88	- 0.9	3.5
1988-89	8.5	11.1
1989-90	10.8	6.0
1990-91	3.4	5.6

Source: DESHP.

Much of the plan outlay has gone to the broad infrastructural development in the earlier years (about 80 per cent of First Five Year Plan). The subsequent plans have allocated more than 60 per cent of its total outlay to build growth potential of the state economy. Despite this the state does lack in high status development of many vital infrastructural development as compared with the other states of India. The problem of unequal distribution within the state is still felt at large. The treatment of infrastructural facilities in respect of population size make the situation appear rather bright but keeping in view the distribution of population and infrastructural facilities which do not go hand in hand makes the situation problem-some and even deteriorating. However, those infrastructure which are distributed according to population like bank, road, schools, hospitals, etc. are considered satisfactory. On this ground one may evaluate the level of development high, but it would be better to take the more safe view that, the more the infrastructure a region has the more development potential it comes to acauire. Thus, a balanced growth to these facilities in Himachal Pradesh, as elsewhere, can prove to be helpful in the future growth of the state economy, provided appropriate policies are adopted by the government to direct the resources into the commodity production sectors which use these facilities as inputs for production of goods and services (Sharma '85).

The factor which explains well the growth of economy in the recent past unlike earlier is the fact that the state has shown slackness in structural change in the economy. Even within sub economy this has been more or less the same over time. However, some structural changes may have recorded intra-sector levels which did not seem to be enough to bring about change in the economy as a whole. And, more so the sectors like industry which have higher factor productivity, have recorded even less change leading to low development in growth potential. The growth actual or potential should have equity in distribution otherwise make growth which may result into accumulation of wealth in certain spatial unit. To evaluate the question of spatial analysis of diversification both the growth actual and potential have been undertaken. The situation that emerges from the spatial analysis explains that the fruits of growth are distributed more equally in Himachal Pradesh but the factors which stem slight out of natural bounty have great diversity. The disparities in income and wealth arising in the plains as a result of the land policies of the British and the recent industrialisation, commercialisation and urbanisation, with their consequent social antagonisms, are largely absent in the hills but agronomic endowment have variation leading to spatial disparity (Sanwal). However, for certain economists the structure of the economy of Himachal Pradesh emerges from the analysis in the following forms: (a) A low poverty ratio as compared to most other states of the country according to nearly all the available estimates; (b) largely improving socio-economic conditions over time of poverty groups like farm labour, and scheduled castes and scheduled tribes; (c) the concentration ratio of asset distribution among rural households being among the lowest in the country in early 1970's and the concentration of ownership of agricultural land falling a little during the 1970s; (d) the concentration ratio of size distribution of consumer expenditure in respect of rural Himachal Pradesh in early 1970s being quite low in itself, and also in comparison to other states of the country.

Another method, apart from the growth habit, agronomic built-up and growth product, is the one which takes accordance of per cent population below poverty line. The composition of population of different unit comprising larger population below poverty line would also exhibit a situation wherein less number of population will be there with enough capital to participate in development process and relegating the region less developed. This, though, would not be useful tool to understand level of development yet can be used for comparative analysis of level of different spatial unit.

Development and problem

The treatment of development exhibits various impediments or specific resistances for a better balanced development. Apart from the variation in agroclimatic factors the uneven distribution of population is of great significance. Certain facilities which are area based, (e.g. electricity supply) become very costly. As in the case of Lahaul and Spiti where the density of population is about two persons per square kilometre it is many times costly to electrify every household as compared to Kangra where return from the higher density zone seems frugal. The small land holdings and their constant decline in size pose another serious problem associated with anthropogenic activity. The fragmentation is even more in areas which have higher density of population leading to decline in productivity and difficulty in adoption of modern farm input. Therefore, greater need is to extend ways through which small land holdings, consequence of both natural topographical and cultural factors, may be put to best agricultural use as it is single most important factor of economic growth in the state. Another factor of great significance is that of great dependency of population on agriculture. The fact that only about 15 per cent of the area is fit for cultivation and there is great pressure on land, as expressed by small holding, there is a need to devise certain structural changes. The under-employed population or the marginal productivity of family labour has begun to act as resistance and any further deployment may prove possible collapse, i.e. activities rendering counter productive generation. Another dimension is added by the studies of J.P. Bhati (1992) that commercial farming (based on fruit and vegetable or both) requires more input from forest and common property resources. Since these resources are already showing signs of degradation, a rapid shift from traditional farming to commercial farming due to latter's 'servicing need' will put more pressure on the natural (vegetation) resources unless some substitute for wood is popularised. Twenty-five per cent to forty per cent of input contribution, from the natural resources sector to the per rupee of output from different farming systems indicate the undiminished role of the commons and the public resources in the farming system in Himachal Pradesh. Structural change unaccompanied by accentuation of inequalities would be needed to preserve and strengthen the relatively egalitarian socio-economic structure. This would require development of activities outside agriculture, though complementary with it, in the rural areas themselves (Sharma '85).

However, taking a lesson from other developed mountain regions of the world, the developmental strategy must aim at practices that act in consonance with environment and blind adoption of economic development mechanism must be eschewed. Social cost of economic development must also be accounted for. The situation should be avoided in which anthropogenic impact leads to negative growth in economy in longer perspective of time.

Agroclimatic zones

Himachal Pradesh has been divided into four agroclimatic zones, keeping in view of the homogeneity shared by each zone in respect of natural factors, viz. topography, altitude, temperature, rainfall, humidity and crop combination. These zones share all or some of the above mentioned characteristics equally within their own boundaries. The four zones are: (1) Low Hill Sub-Tropical Zone, (2) Mid Hill Sub-Humid Zone, (3) High Hill Temperate Wet Zone and (4) High Hill Temperate Dry Zone. Various characteristics of these zones are given in Table 6.2.

Anthronomic system of agroclimatic zones

The ecological set up and the human activities in different agroclimatic zones present an ideal case for their study and identification as typical anthronomic systems. The economic activities of villages (anthronomic-loosely defined) is guided by their requirement and nature's course of yielding. Different set of villages were selected randomly from the four agroclimatic zones to get an insight of the situation. The group of villages were taken to be better reflective of anthronomic activities than unitary as both the number and the chances of diversification got enhanced in the process. The household survey was conducted during 1991-92 in the Chamba Tehsil (High Hill Temperate Wet), Keylong (High Hill Temperate Dry), Bangana Tehsil (Low Hill) and Theog (Mid Hill). The villages where survey was conducted included Salga, Saru and Udaipur Khas in Chamba, Godhla and Purd near Keylong, Hatli Patialan, Rowar and Manjhiani near Bangana in Una district and Jagori, Nalla and Chabtu in Theog near Shimla. Various anthronomic activities were studied to evaluate human impact and levels of development.

Farming system in different zones

Income structure of different zones on household level is a significant indicator to explain the process and level of farm-oriented activities in the predominantly rural areas of Himachal Pradesh. In the low hills a mixed subsistence farming system exists, heavily supported by off-farm income (basically remit-

TABLE 6.2

Characteristic features of agroclimatic zones of H.P.

Features	Low hill zone	Mid hill zone	High hill wet zone	High hill dry zone
(1)	(2)	(3)	(4)	(5)
Altitude (m)	350-650	650-1800	1800-2200	2000-3500
Rainfall (cm)	80-150	150-300	100-150	25 (no crops without irrigation)
Soils	Sandy loam, (poor water retention capacity)	Clay laom (acid and deficient in N)	Shallow, acidic (silt loam, deficient in N and P)	Sandy loam (alkaline and low in fertility)
Population density per km.	230	140-230	60-140	5-60
Cultivated area	37%	25%	30%	30%
Area under forests	14%	40%	23%	7%
Area under pastures	26%	29%	50%	80%
Livestock density/ km. (whole H.P.)	215-220	220	150	35
Livestock density of per km. of forests & pasture land only	542	317	211	40

Contd.

TABLE 6.2 CONTD.

(1)	(2)	(3)	(4)	(5)
Major food crops	Wheat, maize rice, oilseeds sugarcane	Wheat, rice, blackgram, ginger, oil-seeds, pulses, vegetables	Maize, wheat pulses, millets, seed potato, temperate vege-tables, seeds, off-season vegetables	Barley, wheat, buckwheat, pea. seed potato vegetable seeds.
Major problems	Declining land man ratio High pressure on primary activities Water deficit in summer for both drinking and irrigation	Low land-man ratio Lack of fertile plain Irrigation water scarcity	Arable land scarcity Restricted months of cultivation, Irrigation deficiency	Very small growing season, Severe water problem, Lack of loams
Major potential	Season, mild cold, good for double cropping	Season, good for vegetable growth and mix farming local resources based industries	Balance land man ratio, Farm and cash crop growth, cool temperate climate for growth of fruits.	Land pressure of man on land, Dry summer, good climate for best quality seed production of potato etc.

tances). In the mid-hills, a mixed farming system exists, where livestock, farm forestry, vegetables, and off-farm activities are equal contributors to household income. The climate of mid-hill zone is suitable for off-season vegetables and stone fruits. Wherever the weather is favourable and there is easy access to roads and markets, these activities have emerged as the main sources of household income and employment. Hence, in such locations, a farming system based on vegetables and stone fruits has become prominent. As far as type of best crop is concerned fruit cultivation (mainly apples) predominates in the high hill wet zone. In the high hill dry zone, livestock and off-farm activities are the main sources of sustenance. Due to the dominance of commercial crop cultivation the per capita income in the high hill wet zone is much higher than in other zones. The idea of family income structure in different agroclimatic zones can clearly be had from Table 6.3.

Due to unfavourable weather conditions in the high hill dry zone, the productivity of crops is very low (Swarup and Singh 1988). In the low hill zone and the high hill dry zone, the rainfall is low and unreliable making crop cultivation risky, but sometimes it falls with such intensity that it causes soil erosion and imposes expensive burden on soil conservation activities. Farming in the low hill zone and in the high hill dry zone, on the whole, are subject to a greater degree of natural risks than in the mid-hill zone and the high hill wet zone, owing to the greater incidence of droughts and floods. Therefore, the farmers of low hill and the high hill dry zones especially new large capital reserves (but rarely have) to enable them to surmount these disasters. The degree of risk is reduced in some areas by providing irrigation facilities.

Farm families rely on non-farm income and remittances to stabilize their annual incomes and consumption. Moreover, livestock rearing is the only feasible activity where there is uneven relief or a different climate (as in the case of the high hill dry zone) and where food production or the production of

TABLE 6.3

Sourcewise household income in different zones of Himachal Pradesh (sample village figures)

Particular	(Bangana)		(Theog)		(Chamba)		(Keylong)	
	Low hill	(%)	Mid hill	(%)	High hill wet	(%)	High hill dry	(%)
1. Farm Income (fruit, cereal, livestock & vegetables)	12031	46.7	24665	76.7	81071	92.5	11320	56.3
2. Other Income	13706	53.5	7452	23.3	6562	7.5	8783	43.7
3. Total Income	25737	100.00	32117	100.00	87633	100.00	20103	100.00

other agricultural products (e.g. wood) is difficult (Negi 1990, Swarup and Singh 1988). In the high hill temperate dry zone the transhumance farming system is followed, since the resource base is poor and the area remains snow-bound for about six months in a year (November to April), the farmers shift their livestock (sheep and goats) to the lower hills for grazing.

Human resources

Ever since the inception of family planning strategy, Himachal Pradesh has shown indication of adoption and despite being an agrarian economy to the root, it has confined itself to smaller family size. Like the situation in other hills of India in Himachal too, the ratio of working members to total family members is low. The idea of family size, literacy, work force and occupational distribution can be had from Table 6.4. It is clear from this table that households earning substantial

TABLE 6.4

Family size, literacy, workforce and occupational distribution in Himachal Pradesh

Particulars	Low hill zone	Mid hill zone	High hill wet zone	High hill dry zone
Family size (No. of persons)	8*	7	5	8
Literacy (%)	68	72.4	81	52
Work force/ family (No.)	5	4	2	4
Occupational distribution (%)				
Agriculture related	84.2	91.1	92.3	85.9
Service	14.7	17.1	6.0	13.7
Other activities	1.1	1.8	0.9	0.4

Source: Field Survey 1992.

*Persons rounded to nearest figure.

incomes from fruit farming, in the high hill wet zone, have small families, are more literate, have a greater degree of commercialization, and have a higher dependency on farm income, whereas households in the low hill zone and in the high hill dry zone have bigger families, lower income, a lower degree of literacy, and less dependency on farming.

Land holding

Heavy dependence on land, poor consolidation and traditional method of cultivation are some of the factors which have resulted in situation in which Himachal Pradesh records maximum holding size (40 per cent) under marginal (less than 1 hectare) category. The land holding more than 4 hectares is less than 10 per cent if calculated for all the regions of state. However, this is more in mid hill and less in high hill zones. A clear picture of per cent wise land holding distribution can be had from Table 6.5 developed from the field work in different agroclimatic zones of Himachal Pradesh.

TABLE 6.5

Land holding—size and their per cent distribution in different agroclimatic zones of Himachal Pradesh

Holding size	Low hill zone	Mid hill zone	High hill wet zone	High hill dry zone	All zones
Marginal (1 hectare)	24.3	38.50	66.1	56.4	40.0
Small (1-2 hectares)	29.7	21.15	16.9	23.0	24.4
Medium (2-4 hectares)	35.2	27.75	10.4	15.0	25.3
Large (4 hectares)	10.8	12.55	2.6	6.6	9.8
Average holding size	2.19	2.25	1.00	1.25	1.67

Source: Adopted from J.P. Bhati et. al. and personal computation.

The proportion of marginal size land holding to total holding is higher in the high hill zone than in the low hill zone and in the mid-hill zone. The proportion of marginal-size farms is 24 per cent in the low hill zone and 38.5 per cent in the mid-hill zone. The proportion of large holdings (i.e. holdings above 4 hectares) varies from 3 to 13 per cent of the total holdings in all the zones. Nevertheless, the over-whelming majority of land holdings fall under small and marginal farm categories.

Modern farm input

There has been a very strong positive correlation between commercialisation and high input in terms of fertilizer, developed seeds and plant protection materials. The annual application of these materials in all different agroclimatic zones which can be seen in Table 6.6 as was observed during field survey.

TABLE 6.6

Annual application of modern inputs in different agroclimatic zones in H.P.

Input	Low hill zone	Mid hill zone	High hill wet zone	High hill dry zone
1. Fertilizer (kg./hectare)	20-60	160	200-320	20
2. Developed seeds (% area)				
Wheat	99	100	95	98
Paddy	85	89	80	85
Maize	35	90	40	40
3. Plant Protection material (Rs./ha)	10	300	3000	50

Source: Field Survey.

The high yielding varieties require more modern input and a relationship of these two can be seen in the above table. The high hill wet zone which also specialises in apple plantation and commercialisation recorded maximum input of such commodities.

Livestock resources

The density and composition of livestock is another indicator which can be studied to explain the diversity level of climatic adaptation and agro-economic structure of various agroclimatic zones of Himachal Pradesh. The study of villages in different agroclimatic zones and livestock structure was done at household level. It was observed that bigger animals are common in commercial agriculture zone whereas goat or sheep are common in drier parts where grazing land is scarce and stall feed is costly. In the high hill wet zone due to competition with other agricultural activities like orchard managing, it is noted that it forbids farmers from keeping livestock (Table 6.7).

TABLE 6.7

Livestock resources composition in different agroclimatic zones of Himachal Pradesh

Type of livestock	Low hill	Mid hill	High hill wet	High hill dry
1. Cattle	6.03	5.70	2.46	5.31
2. Buffalo	1.18	1.41	—	—
3. Sheep & Goat	4.13	1.13	0.04	81.94
4. Yaks	—	—	—	0.30
5. Mules & others	—	0.06	—	0.45
Total livestock	11.34	8.30	2.50	88.00

Source: Field Survey '92 and developed from Bhati et.al.

Except for the high hill dry zone, the number of large animals in the livestock possessed by farmers, is higher in all farming systems. Both manure and draft power are important necessitating the possession of large animals. Under each of these systems a few small animals (sheep and goats) are also kept by farmers to meet their clothing and meat requirements and also as an asset that can easily be sold at times of emergency. Overstocking of animals and denudation of common grazing resources are two main problems of the livestock sector in the region.

The varied treatment of development level evaluation in relation to anthropogenic impact exhibit the close relationship between natural factors and level differential.. The different levels coincide with the agroclimatic division and their consideration acquires permanent significance for extension of developmental strategy. The four agroclimatic regions are also four units from the view point of prospect of development. The differential population also having agroclimatic reflection houses unequal infrastructural built-up and treatment of development levels only on administrative spatial basis has its own limitations. Hence development in most of the cases have been evaluated from the population point of view also, accommodating the variation in anthronomic parameters.

References

Arora, C., Development of Agriculture and Allied Sector, 1976.

Basu, K. The Less Developed Economy: A Critique of Contemporary Theory, Oxford University Press, 1984.

Census of India 1971, 1981, 1991.

Census of India, District Census Handbook (for different districts and years).

Chattopadhya, B.C., Emerging Concept of Rural Development and Planning, 1979.

Chenery, Hollis and Syrquin, M., Pattern of Development 1950-70, Oxford University Press, London, 1975.

DESHP, Statistical Abstract (for different districts and years).

DESHP, Statistical Outline of Himachal Pradesh.

Donald McGraham, 'Development Indicators and Models', *Journal of Development Studies*, April 1972.

Draft Tribal Subplan, Tribal Development, H.P. Govt. Publication.

Economic Review of Himachal Pradesh (yearly information), H.P. Govt.

Gay, Hunter, Modernising Peasant Societies: A Comparative Study in Asia, Oxford University Press, London, 1969.

Harbinson, F. and Myers, C.A., Education, Manpower and Economic Growth—Strategies of Human Resource Development, McGraw Hill Book Company, New York, 1964.

Harry, W. Richardson, Regional and Urban Economics, Penguin, 1978.

Hebsur, R.K., 'Modernization, Mobilization and Rural Development', *Indian Journal of Social Work*, 39(4), 1979.

Himachal Pradesh Census Atlas 1971, 1981, 1991, Government of India.

Kaur, J., Himalayan Pilgrims and the New Tourism, Himalayan Books, 1978.

Kaushal, R.K., Himachal Pradesh: Socio-economic, Geographical and Historical Survey, Reliance Publishing House, New Delhi.

Kayastha, S.L. and Khurana, V.K., Geographical and Environmental Approach for Integrated Rural Development, *The Journal of Scientific Research*, Vol. XXIX (2).

Khan, A.R. and Singh, R.B., 'Human Resources Base for Rural Development in a Mountainous Region' in Ashok Kumar (ed.) Human Resource Development, Anmol Publications, 1991.

Khan, A.R. and Singh, R.B.: 'Micro Level Monitoring of Landuse and Agriculture in Himalayas' in Noor Mohammad (ed.) New Dimension in Agricultural Geography, Vol. 4, 1992.

Mehta, M.M., Human Resource Development Planning with special reference to Asia and the Far East, The Macmillan Company of India, 1976.

Mukherjee, A. B., 'Agricultural Region and Geographical Planning for Indian Agriculture', *National Geographer*, 1962.

Planning Commission, Government of India, 5th, 6th and 7th Plans.

Sanwal, M., 'Design of Hill Development: Lessons for the Plan of Uttar Pradesh and Himachal Pradesh', *Economic and Political Weekly*, February 1983.

Shashi, S.S., Himachal Pradesh—Nature's Peaceful Paradise, ISSD Publication, New Delhi.

Singh, J., An Agricultural Atlas of India: A Geographical Analysis, 1974.

Swarup, R. and Sikka, B.K., Agricultural Development in Himachal Pradesh, Agricole Publishing Agency, New Delhi, 1983.

Index